WALKING TO DESTINY

11 Actions an Owner **MUST** Take to Rapidly Grow Value & Unlock Wealth

CHRISTOPHER M. SNIDER

Copyright © 2016 Christopher M. Snider
All rights reserved. No part of this book may be reproduced or transmitted in any form or by any means, electronic or mechanical, including photocopying, recording, or by any information storage and retrieval system currently in use or invented in the future without the prior written permission of the author, except for the inclusion of brief quotations in critical reviews and certain other non-commercial uses permitted by copyright law. For permission requests, contact the publisher.

ThinkTank Publishing House
A Division of Snider Premier Growth
14701 Detroit Avenue | Suite 430
Cleveland, Ohio 44107

Library of Congress Control Number: 2016907518
ISBN 978-0-9972527-0-5 (paperback)
ISBN 978-0-9972527-2-9 (hardcover)

Editing and Proofreading by Brooke Norman
Cover and Interior Design by Codesign LLC
Printed by Marquis

Distributed by Snider Value Index
www.SniderValueIndex.com

To place orders through Snider Value Index:
Tel: (216) 712-4244
Email: Books@SniderValueIndex.com

Large discounts are available for bulk orders.
Please contact Brooke Norman at (216) 712-4244
or visit www.WalkingToDestiny.com

Printed in Canada

TO MY PEERS:

BABY BOOMER BUSINESS OWNERS, THE TRUE CHANGE AGENTS WHO BUILT A WORLD WORTH VALUING.

Acknowledgements

I dedicate this book to business owners. You are the risk-takers, the visionaries, the game-changers who propel a society forward. You are your business and because of that, it becomes a true expression of your talent, passion, and hard work. I, like you, am a business owner to my core. And ultimately, I wrote this book to acknowledge your unparalleled contributions to the market and to invest in your successful transition to the next big thing you will go on to do.

I have learned that writing a book is quite a taxing project and it could not have been accomplished without the support of my family, including my lovely wife of 34 wonderful years, Denice; my brilliant and creative daughter, Ashley; my soon-to-be son-in-law, Dan; and my son, Scott Snider, who is more than a son to me. Scott is my business partner and my best friend. I am so blessed to have a son, partner, and friend who believes in me so much.

I would like to thank my clients, past and present, for the experiences we have shared throughout the book. I'd also like to thank the many mentors I have been inspired by, particularly "Uncle Freddie," Phil Andrews, Andy Rayburn, and Peter Christman, for their patience and wisdom, which now, approaching my third act and looking back, I appreciate more than ever.

Thank you to Brian Frolo and the team at Codesign, our book designer, for working through the many changes in both content and timelines. A big thanks to Sean Hutchinson and Scott Miller for providing their insights and for the friendship and belief in the cause we have chosen to pursue together; to the Exit Planning Institute (EPI) faculty, board, and members whose content and expertise are changing outcomes for business owners and their families; and to the staff at Snider Premier Growth and EPI, Christina Metz, Josh Koza, and most of all, Kimberly "Brooke" Norman, all of whom work tirelessly on behalf of the members of our family enterprise.

This project was Brooke's first major undertaking since joining the team at Snider Premier Growth. She worked around the clock, dedicating many personal hours to assembling all the edits, gently nudging me to keep us on track, and helping me express my voice in this book. She was my collaborative accountability buddy, and through this experience we have developed a friendship that will last forever. Thank you, Brooke! This could not have been accomplished without you, and I swear I will make it up to you.

Lastly, I couldn't have written this book without having a place to go to retreat from the distractions of the day-to-day and "brain dump." Thank you to Bowman's Beach Park for that picnic table in the sun.

Contents

FOREWORD BY SCOTT SNIDER IX
THE PURPOSE OF THIS BOOK VX
THE PERFECT EXIT XVII

SECTION ONE: You and Your Business | Embracing the Changing Times 1
    Chapter 1: The Times They Are A-Changin' 3
    Chapter 2: The Baby Boomer Business Owner 13
    Chapter 3: Every Hero Has a Flaw 27
    Chapter 4: Changing Your Paradigm 43

SECTION TWO: Core Concepts of Value Acceleration 53
    Chapter 5: The Three Legs of the Stool 55
    Chapter 6: Value ~~Versus~~ AND Income 69
    Chapter 7: The Four C's 87
    Chapter 8: Relentless Execution 107

SECTION THREE: How to Implement Value Acceleration 133
    Chapter 9: Gate One | DISCOVER — The Triggering Event 135
    Chapter 10: Gate One | DISCOVER — Creating Action Plans 173
    Chapter 11: Gate Two | PREPARE — Delivering Action Plans 199
    Chapter 12: Gate Three | DECIDE — Grow or Sell? 211

SECTION FOUR: Walking to Destiny 227
    Chapter 13: Changing Your Outcome 229
    Conclusion 260

APPENDIX 261
    Exhibits 262
    Recommended Reading List 264
    Public Speaking 266
    Voice of the Industry 267

Foreword

I've known Chris Snider for 30 years. For 15 of those years, I have called him my mentor and teacher. For 10 of them, I have called him my business partner. And for all 30 of them, I have had the honor of calling him my friend and father. Uniquely, I have had the opportunity to be alongside Chris, experiencing the many different hats he may wear on any given day. I have seen him at the top, and I have seen him at the bottom.

The best way I can describe Chris is not just through his business accomplishments, or the countless lessons I have learned from him, or even the person he is in his personal life. He is more than that.

Chris Snider is *the* leader; for our family, for our companies, and for the industry. Chris is, very simply, the guy who drives the car when everyone else needs to sleep.

I started my first company at the age of 17 and grew that company with mentorship and support from Chris. In 2010, I decided to sell that company. Thankfully, I had a dad who was an exit planner and value acceleration specialist. I spent the late spring and summer of 2010 transitioning that company to the new owners and integrating it into their organization. At the same time, Chris asked me to join his consulting firm, Aspire Management. And so in the fall of 2010, I did that.

I started by becoming an analyst. I would analyze tax documents, recast financial statements, prepare the Enterprise Value Assessment reports for the team, review industries and comparables for the valuation analysis and, eventually, build the company book.

It was in early 2011 that Chris brought me into his office and said, "Scott, I want to be **THE** exit planner in Northeast Ohio. When owners and advisors think about building value and transitioning their companies, I want them to think of me. Can you do that for me?"

At the time I was 25 years old, was new to this industry, and had absolutely no technical experience whatsoever. I suppose the entrepreneurial, challenge-seeking, competitive spirit that burns inside me took over and I responded by saying, "Yes, absolutely!"

What I didn't anticipate, or really have any idea of at all, was the magnitude that very simple answer would have for our future; that we had stepped onto a path to become the nationally recognized authority in exit planning and value acceleration.

I started by analyzing all of Chris's materials, workshops, processes, and philosophies. What I knew was that he had a pretty diverse career—working with major international corporations all the way down to small family businesses. And that within those organizations, he had a diverse career path—from auditor to systems implementer to supply chain manager at Sherwin Williams, to logistics, *then* over to consulting for Price Waterhouse, *then* leaping over to being an executive at a nuts and bolts distributor, *then* running a multi-billion-dollar division as CIO for Textron. He got into IT, websites, and content marketing and eventually started his own consulting firm.

All of that robust experience, when you really analyze it and boil it down, equated to helping owners and their executive teams grow their companies, manage and execute projects, and lead teams.

Chris had something unique. I think if you ask Chris why he started his consulting firm, he would answer that it was to challenge himself to convert all that experience and knowledge into action for any size of company to create successful results. Would it work?

Chris also had a concept entitled *BIGS: Buy, Improve, Grow, Sell*. It was a process, but to me, it was really more of a workshop series that existed inside something bigger. It was when I started digging through some of his sales binders, presentations, and white papers that I discovered he had organized the "something bigger" into a single process. I remember talking to Chris about this content and telling him he needed to take the time to build it into one system or methodology that we could follow and take owners through. He already had all that robust, diverse knowledge and experience. It just needed to be fully developed. I envisioned that finished methodology appearing right on the front page of our Aspire Management website. I wanted it to be a core part of who we were and what we did. So Chris and I took the time to sit down and articulate the exact process he would utilize with a business owner who was focused on growing enterprise value, with the intent of always being prepared for an exit. What emerged was significant. Chris had created what we know today as, the Value Acceleration Methodology™.

Parallel to this path, we were also walking an entirely different one. As we worked on developing Aspire Management, we also wrote the business plan for a family investment firm, made up of Chris and me, with the mission of investing in small businesses where we could not only invest capital, but invest our expertise and knowledge as well. This venture would become Snider Premier Growth (SPG).

So the Value Acceleration Methodology was in place, our consulting firm was rebranded and remodeled, and it was going well. Clients not only showed interest, but we had success in using the Methodology.

Then came the Exit Planning Institute (EPI). Chris was a member of EPI before he was the owner, holding the Certified Exit Planning Advisor (CEPA) designation since 2008. However, we believed that exit planning needed clearer definition and more of a practical process. We knew that exit planning was actually just good business strategy, driven by focusing on building enterprise value and complemented by aligning business, personal, and financial goals (a concept now called Master Planning, created by Peter Christman). With the acquisition of EPI, we could bring the Methodology full circle and teach it to fellow advisors and CEPAs across the nation. It was something our industry and marketplace was lacking, and it was much needed. It defined what exit strategy really was and provided a practical system to execute. In the fall of 2012, we purchased EPI and by the fall of 2013, the Value Acceleration Methodology was the core curriculum taught throughout the CEPA Program. In fact, it quickly became the most recognized and widely adopted system in the exit planning industry.

The last part of my Value Acceleration Methodology story lives within our own Snider companies. You might be reading this and saying to yourself, "If this methodology is so successful, do *you* actually use it at your companies?"

The answer is a definitive yes. Now in 2016, SPG owns eight different companies, which all live and breathe Value Acceleration.

It's an interesting time for me. Chris has now stepped forward to concentrate on writing, speaking, teaching, and building content. And I have stepped into Chris' shoes, leading our companies and teams using the value growth system I helped create. The business has certainly come full circle, and so have I. From helping Chris write the Value Acceleration Methodology to teaching it to our CEPAs at the Exit Planning Institute, and now living it every day with my team here at Snider Premier Growth.

As you read about Value Acceleration in this book, you will find that it has become much more than just a process. It has become the best-practice management system. It is the appropriate way to run and build successful companies. It is your roadmap to an eventual transition. It is your bodyguard for unplanned events. It prepares you. It's tool you can use to engage your employees and build a culture of ownership and entrepreneurism. It's a process that integrates business, personal, and financial goals and aligns them equally. It is the vehicle to harness and harvest wealth. It's a project management tool. It is a *proven* process that, if followed correctly, will increase the value of your business, and (perhaps more importantly) give you as the owner a sound financial plan, a vision for the future, and passion for life-after-business. At the very minimum, Value Acceleration will change the way the business owner thinks… the way you think.

So, Chris Snider: the family man, the business man, the corporate executive, the entrepreneur, the teacher, speaker, writer, and consultant. An average golf buddy, and my best friend. A man with many hats, many roles, and a lot of wisdom. Chris is a true visionary. He is a pioneer for the industry and helping to create and change a marketplace.

After reading this book, I challenge you as an advisor to think about how this process will change your business, how it may help you better engage your clients, and how it will help them grow and transition their companies. You can be a key part of all of that with them.

For you, the owner, I challenge you to think about the immense ways these actions will change your business and life. I challenge you to embrace the opportunity of building value and planning personally and financially.

It's certainly not an easy road, but if you embrace these concepts and truly integrate them into your daily practice and operations, it will change your life, both professionally and personally. It certainly has mine.

—Scott Snider, Vice President of Exit Planning Institute and Operating Partner of Snider Premier Growth

The Purpose of This Book

> "By thought, the thing you want is brought to you; by action, you receive it."
> —Wallace Wattles, *The Science of Getting Rich*

SIMPLY, MY PURPOSE IS TO EMPOWER YOU.

Your relationship to your business has a life cycle. By starting, buying, or owning your business, you have set yourself on a path. This path is leading you and your business toward your eventual exit. It is a fact. There will come a time when your most valuable asset will change hands. You will cease to be the owner. Whether that transition is successful is up to you.

I named this book after a gospel song entitled "Walking In My Destiny."

Gospel music is spiritually uplifting; I like to listen to it while running or when I need a little inspiration. *Walking In My Destiny* suggests we all have a destiny within our reach, and with faith, we will achieve it. Faith is confidence or trust in a person or thing; the observance of an obligation from loyalty; fidelity to a person, promise, engagement; or a belief not based on proof.

I want you to unlock the wealth trapped in your business prior to your imminent exit and create the future and legacy you deserve. It is your destiny to grow the value of your most significant asset, harvest those riches, and enter the best act of your life. This book is designed to give you the knowledge of value acceleration and exit planning necessary to take deliberate steps on your walk to destiny.

This is a book written for business owners by a business owner. Despite my years of consulting, I still view myself as an owner more than anything else. On top of that, I have evolved into the role of an educator and have found real passion in that. I felt compelled to write a book to arm fellow business owners with the knowledge and understanding to recognize their potential and actually know how to execute tactics to grow and harvest the wealth locked in their businesses. It is also designed to bridge the understanding gap between advisors (who I train) and owners (who I am) and get them on the same page. I can tell you from an advisor perspective that the Value Acceleration Methodology has become the leading process for exit planning and is prominently utilized by exit planning advisors across the world. It's a proven system to maximize value, grow income, and build a business that can run without you, even if you never plan to leave. Though I think you are naïve if you think you won't ever exit your business, the business owner who never plans to leave needs a well-functioning, attractive business more than anyone.

I want to change the outcome for business owners who have invested their lives in their business. To do that, I need to change the paradigm of how exit planning is perceived by owners. Exit planning is good business strategy. Exit planning is now.

With readiness comes success, freedom, and wealth, and providing that roadmap on your walk to destiny is the purpose of my book.

The Perfect Exit

MY CAREER AS A CHANGE AGENT AND THE HISTORY OF THE VALUE ACCELERATION METHODOLOGY

I have been working in the realm of business improvements for nearly 35 years. My first role as a value accelerator was after graduating from John Carroll University, when I became an operational auditor for The Sherwin Williams Company (SW), headquartered in Cleveland, Ohio. Auditors arrived at stores and commercial branches unannounced, showed our IDs, and asked to count the cash. One of an auditor's jobs is to catch people who are stealing from the company, and I caught my fair share. The real role of the auditor is to prevent theft. Most people steal because they think they have the *opportunity* to steal. Auditors are around to let people know that someone is checking so those who *thought* they had the opportunity would think twice about it.

When I found something wrong, I would "write up" the store. Managers hated to be written up, especially by a 22-year-old kid who knew little about how to actually operate a store. While that was true for me in the beginning, each auditor was given an "Audit Guide" (structural capital), which spelled out how we were to conduct our reviews and what to look for. I wasn't there to interpret the rules; I was there to ensure compliance to the rules.

However, we were also encouraged to listen to the store manager's suggestions and complaints. If we saw something that did not make sense, we were encouraged to challenge the norm, bring it up to the audit manager, and make suggestions for improvements. Coming up with ideas to make things better put you on the fast track for promotion. Anybody could follow an audit guide. But making suggestions on how to improve operations was how you got ahead. It's how you stood out as more than just an enforcer. We actually had buttons that we wore on our lapels that read "We're Here to Help." That always got a big laugh from the store and commercial managers. But in the big picture, that's what we were really there to do.

Store and commercial branch managers didn't trust auditors at first. But once you built a reputation in your territory as someone who could make things better, you became a bridge to getting things changed back at corporate. And the Audit department could do that. We carried a lot of weight at SW.

This became even more important once I returned to Cleveland and started doing corporate audits. I audited all kinds of different departments—from Workers Comp to Purchasing to manufacturing plants and distribution centers. The Audit department was the proving ground for advancement at SW. It was like a boot camp for future division managers. Within about three years, you either graduated to a position in one of the divisions or you were out. SW used the Audit department to screen and build talent that it could send to the divisions (human capital).

I graduated from Audit to join the Purchasing department in 1985, where I introduced the use of the first PC. Boy, I could tell you stories about these first computers that both young and old readers would find amusing. If you are over 55, you probably have a few yourself. Anyway, just let me say... the computer has come a *very* long way since 1985. I put the first budget on the computer and my boss was simply amazed at the productivity advantages of the PC. He ordered me to "get one of those things on every desk in this department" after he saw what it could do.

Now having the reputation of being the so-called "computer whiz" guy (which I really was not—I knew how to do spreadsheets using Lotus 123), I was selected to be on a full-time team called IBA (Integrated Business

Applications) to implement Enterprise Resource Planning (ERP) systems at all SW plants. That led to numerous other special projects, like designing and implementing the first inbound freight system used by SW and, one of my favorites, the Batch Tracking Project (BTP). BTP is still one of my most cherished experiences to this day.

SW was growing and the Morrow, Georgia, plant was reaching capacity. Several of us believed that ERP systems, specifically Shop Floor Control, if used properly, could increase plant capacity by 20%, with little to no increase in space or equipment, by improving the flow of manufacturing through the plant. The capital investment savings to SW would be enormous if we could prove this true. Many, at both corporate and the plant, doubted it.

My boss and mentor at the time, Fred Ristow, or "Uncle Freddie" as we affectionately called him, was a 42-year veteran at SW. He helped me take the idea to the president and VP of Manufacturing. I asked for six months and my pick of any two IT guys to go to Morrow with me to show them it could be done.

The plant manager was so against it, he put up a sign the first day I arrived at the plant entrance. It read "Chris Snider, You Now Have 180 Days Left." Every day, he would update the countdown: "Chris Snider, You Now Have 179 Days Left. Chris Snider, You Now Have 178 Days Left." After a few months, he began to see we were making progress and took the sign down. Six months after that, he was handing me an award. His results were so improved that the other plant managers were calling him, asking him what he was doing. When he told them it was this "system" they installed, all the plant managers started asking for it. It was eventually rolled out to all the plants.

Bear in mind, it wasn't just the system. Systems don't solve problems. People do. You will learn as you read this book that systems are important. But more important were the people, including my team; the guys on the floor; and staff in the plant office such as the purchasing manager, the plant scheduler, and the controller.

A key part of our success was the bond we built with the guys on the floor. Each member of my team had to go work on the shop floor for two weeks. Just imagine the fun the floor guys had with the corporate guys. It was all in good fun, and at the end of the day, they respected that we would get out there on their turf and make paint. We did many of these kinds of activities to build teamwork and demonstrate our respect for the team on the floor. I would meet the first-shift supervisors for breakfast at the Waffle House at 6 a.m. to pick their brains and bond with them. I asked a lot of questions. One of the things I realized from this was that the people who were on the floor knew what needed to be done. All you really needed to do was respect them first, then ask a lot of questions. But it couldn't be superficial. First they needed to trust you, and then they were more than willing to help. Working out on the floor with them was one of the big steps toward earning their respect, removing the threat, and demonstrating sincerity. It worked.

In a post-project review with SW's president, I told him I had learned two very important lessons: 1) put people in positions where they will be successful, and 2) create a culture where change thrives.

After completing that project, I considered starting my own consulting business for the first time. But I was nervous about it. From my experiences at SW, I knew how to successfully implement change, but what did I really know about running a consulting business? Feeling like it was time to see what was going on in the rest of the world, I chose to join Price Waterhouse (PwC) as an "experienced hire" to learn about consulting and branch out.

There I met a wonderful new mentor, Phil Andrews: a gritty, tough, really smart SOB. Phil took me under his wing and we did several projects together. It was Phil who first introduced me to the gating process. Gates represented project transitions. You proceeded through a "gate" only if you met certain criteria. Clarifying these criteria was really important. It forced you to articulate the deliverables or accomplishments that were needed to proceed through the gate to keep a project on track. It also forced accountability. I have developed some form of gating process in almost every situation since, including the gates defined in the Value Acceleration Methodology.

I likened my days at PwC to getting my MBA. PwC taught me the science behind methodology and process improvement through the deployment and engagement of people in change. PwC invested heavily in training and education. During my unbillable time, I attended classes on management, change management, engagement management, and project management. I then had opportunities to apply this new knowledge on projects. That's when I learned that change starts with education, but that education alone is not enough. Real learning comes when you apply that education to real-life situations; that is, only through the educated action are things improved.

From PwC, I joined Roadway Logistics (ROLS), which you know today as FedEx Logistics. The best part of that job was that it was a blend of the implementation experiences I learned at SW and the really creative consulting solutions of PwC. We would not only recommend logistics solutions, but then we had to implement them to make money. In other words, we only ate what we killed. The best part of that experience was the team chemistry.

One of the groups they gave me to manage was in a row of cubicles along the windows. This group was an outcast. That row of cubicles was labeled in the office as "Depression Row." They were rebellious and outspoken. They also happened to be the best project implementers in the company. I can clearly remember one of my first days sitting at the computer in my cubicle with my back to the opening. All of a sudden, someone walked in, stood behind me, and yelled, "I am getting screwed over and I don't like it!" I slowly turned around to see it was one of the managers from Depression Row.

"Hold on," I said. "Calm down; what's going on?" He began to rail about how the management team was interfering with his project and screwing it all up. "They don't know what the h*** they are doing! Why can't they just stay out of my way and let me do my job?" he asked.

I got him calmed down and had him explain the situation. Then I went to the director's office and got them to back off; stop butting in. I told them that we knew what we were doing and we accepted responsibility for the deliverable. Honestly, I was not really sure. But putting my faith in Depression Row showed my team I was ready to back them up. I told them that if we delivered, nobody would mess with us. They might disagree with our methods, but success would trump that. However, if we didn't deliver, we would be dead meat.

That group on Depression Row ended up being the best project management group I ever managed. All they really needed was a voice who could keep the management team at bay while they did their jobs. They were, in reality, a really talented group of change agents. They just needed management to leave them alone and let them do their jobs. They were creative and ambitious; they were doers; they were fighters. And they needed someone to believe in them.

The business was growing so fast we could have 40 projects going at one time, ranging between transportation, warehousing, order management, or all three, which we called integrated. We designed and implemented a "Gateway" process there to keep all these projects going.

Every Monday, between ten o'clock and noon, we would hold a "Gateway Meeting," where project managers would present their stage deliverable to the Gateway Council and either receive approval to proceed to the next stage of the project (through the gate) or be asked to gather additional information. The Gateway team was made up of managers from IT, Marketing, and Operations. They would review the project for its quality of approach, consistency with other projects and customer solutions, consistency with company strategy, and probability of success.

The entire company was always invited because it was the one place that if you really wanted to know what was going on, you could find out. We always had a full room. We created a matrix of solutions along the one end (i.e. transportation, order management, warehousing, integrated) and size along the other. We then predefined solutions at the intersection of each point on the matrix. That allowed us to create reusable solutions that could be predictably and consistently implemented while keeping maintenance costs down.

One day, I got a call from a recruiter. I took the interview at (what was to me at the time) a small ($90M) JIT distributor called Flexalloy (or Flex, as we called it). Little did I know that this interview would change my life, my professional direction, and my family forever.

There I worked for a man named Andy Rayburn. No words can convey the spirit of this man.

If there ever was a perfect exit, it was the exit engineered by Andy Rayburn. I was very fortunate to be part of it. Funny thing is, I didn't know it at the time. I was just happy to part of a great team in a great company, building value, having fun, and enjoying our culture.

In my initial interview, Andy explained that he wanted to grow the company to $250 million in the next three years. He described his vision and really inspired me. He didn't say anything about wanting to sell the company. But we did sell a little more than two years after I joined. Andy made so much money that he was able to start his own private equity company with the proceeds.

To give you an idea of Andy's character, every single employee received a payout based on their level and years with the company. I heard that Andy paid out $10 million to his employees after the sale. It was amazing to see all the new cars in the parking lot two weeks after the payout.

What made Flex so unique that it would sell at such a premium? You have to remember that we were a fastener company: nuts and bolts. When you think of a fastener manufacturer and distribution company, what image comes to mind? It's probably correct. When I first joined the company, to get to my office, you came in the front door, walked through the main office and into the factory, out another door, followed the black trail in the carpet down a long hall, and then turned left. There you would have found several IT people working on card tables... yep, that's what I said. Card tables. In fact, my first desk was a card table. I can vividly remember, standing and looking out the window one day, wondering why I left Price Waterhouse. That, of course, would all change.

Soon we moved to a beautiful new facility in the woods, with ponds and walking trails, a full outdoor basketball court, a 50-yard flag football field, and musical rocks at the entrance of the building. Andy was building a brand experience, and it rubbed off on the partners. Imagine the reaction of customers and suppliers as they parked near the pond and heard Grateful Dead playing in the landscaping as they approached the building. This was not your typical fastener company. The whole company was jazzed. Andy knew everyone's name. He personally helped many who, at some point in their lives, needed it.

Flex did not have an HR department. We had a "Partner Development" department. Every employee was a partner. I know this sounds corny and if it's not real, it *is* corny. But at Flex, it was real. Each month, we would have an In-The-Paint meeting, which was a total company meeting. Every Flex facility had a basketball key painted in it somewhere. Every month, all employees would gather "in the paint" and we would share company-wide success stories. Andy would communicate our plans, our numbers, and pump everyone up. Yes, we actually had a cheer. For me, coming out of the corporate environment, this was amazing. I had only read about companies like this in books. Now, I was here. And on top of that, I was one of the leaders.

In addition to building a brand unlike any other in the industry, we were building a culture and a management team that could run the business without Andy (social capital). We were investing heavily in systems; 2% of revenue went to IT each year. Andy knew that if the sales came as fast as he thought our sales team could deliver, he would need scalable systems. He knew things would need to change. And the sales did come. They came fast and furious. We almost tripled sales in just three years. My role was to implement the systems and help the company grow and evolve. And I brought in my team from Depression Row to help.

During this period of growth, Andy's income did not grow as fast as revenue. There was a lot of pressure and cash flow challenges, but think of the value we were creating! We had five bidders on the business and selected the largest manufacturer in the industry to buy us. They paid dearly. They wanted to sell more of their fasteners to our customers and get us out of the way (customer capital). But even more than that, they were 20 times our size and they couldn't help but imagine the synergies that could be created if they could leverage Flex's customer relationships, purchasing power, culture, processes, and systems.

After the sale, I was immediately promoted by the new corporate owners. But after about a year and a half, I knew I didn't fit into the corporate culture anymore. All this talk of strategy and no action frustrated me. We were cutting, not building. That was not my thing and I was very uncomfortable with it. I had always been part of growth cultures. Now, the culture shifted. It wasn't the same fast-paced, empowered, action-oriented culture anymore. It was just about the numbers now. Not surprising, as we were now part of a public company. It wasn't fun for any of us who were used to the other way of doing things. Within two years, every director was gone. Andy was the first person out the door. I wasn't far behind.

After Flex, I wondered if that experience could ever be duplicated. This became a quest for me. And I wondered if what I learned over all these years improving middle market companies and big corporations could be scaled to leverage effectively in a small business.

Over the next five years, I led two technology companies which doubled and tripled in sales over two- and three-year periods. I learned a lot about small business working for these privately held companies, and a lot about myself. One of the positive things that came from those experiences was proof that what I learned in middle market and big companies *could* be scaled to small business. It was at that point I knew I had a model that worked.

As you can see, the Value Acceleration Methodology didn't form overnight. In fact, from the time I took my first job at Sherwin Williams as a process auditor and onward throughout my career, I have been laser focused on business value improvements that optimize processes, lower costs, invest in future growth, and maximize income.

In 2006, I formed Aspire Management. Through Aspire, I developed a service model called *BIGS* (short for: Buy, Improve, Grow, Sell) which integrates both value growth and transactional services. BIGS is still being offered today. I originally created this model for my son and me, never intending to sell it as a service. I was convinced that the only way to accelerate my wealth was by equity through business ownership. And after two failed attempts to trade services for equity, I was further convinced that the only way I would be able to do it was to acquire my own businesses and apply the BIGS model. As a former COO and CEO, I wanted to develop a holistic growth model that reflected the CEO or owner's point of view. And I wanted to be a business owner and have a system in place that would allow me to work with my son to develop his business skills.

The success of the BIGS model eventually led to the formation of Snider Premier Growth (SPG), a family investment company which now oversees controlling or minority interests in eight companies, some of which I've invested in with clients. It also led to my obtaining the Certified Exit Planning Advisor (CEPA) designation in 2008 and to the 2012 acquisition of the Exit Planning Institute (EPI), an organization providing training and resources to advisors who serve business owners.

The Value Acceleration Methodology is a management system to benchmark your company, identify value drivers (and value killers), deploy action plans to address areas of growth, and revisit the same question every 90 days: Do I continue to grow or do I want to sell? This includes a set of tools and a solid team, with you at the center.

Expanding further, I'd say Value Acceleration is actually a life-planning management system you can use to make the timing of your exit irrelevant. It doesn't require a focus on the "end game." It focuses on *now*. What can I do today to make my business more valuable? You don't have to choose between today and the future. Doing the right things today ensures a successful exit in the future.

Exit planning is grounded in action. A plan gets you nothing if you can't execute. It is only through action that we can create the life we seek and harvest the value of our businesses. There are thousands of books about exit planning and value growth. You get great information and laundry lists of what you can do. You picked up this book, so I'm guessing you've read many of them. But as an owner, I want you to know *how to do it*. I can teach you how to integrate the system and internalize the methods into what you do every day. Then you will have all the pieces you need to truly maximize your performance and become a best-in-class business.

SECTION ONE

You and Your Business: Embracing the Changing Times

In the first section of this book, you will review the story of you: the Baby Boomer business owner. Explore the compelling case for value acceleration and exit planning, and why it is imperative to evolve your mindset. Take a look at the impact Baby Boomers have had over the last 60 years. Review the market trends that prove that exit planning is needed now. Explore the 11 actions you need to accomplish to create a successful business today and a successful exit in your future.

CHAPTER ONE

The Times They Are A-Changin'

For Baby Boomer business owners, exit planning is the number one business and personal challenge of our time. Over the next 10 to 20 years, we will likely see an unprecedented set of business exits. How ready are we as owners? Statistically speaking, not very. Something keeps us from approaching this area of business strategy.

It is an inevitable, undeniable fact that your business will change hands. We all intend and hope that our transition will occur on our timeline and on our terms. But it's just as likely—a 50/50 chance, in fact—that it won't. The late Leon Danco, America's expert on perpetuation and continuity of family-owned business and the author of *Beyond Survival: A Guide for Business Owners and Their Families*, wrote, "Failure to provide for the perpetuity of your business beyond your working lifetime means simply that you have overstated your profits, for when you go, the whole company goes with you."

The Times They Are A-Changin'
Bob Dylan

Come gather 'round people
Wherever you roam
And admit that the waters
Around you have grown
And accept it that soon
You'll be drenched to the bone
If your time to you
Is worth savin'
Then you better start swimmin'
Or you'll sink like a stone
For the times they are a-changin'

Why aren't owners more proactive? The exit from your company represents the harvest of your wealth from the business itself, which is most likely your most significant financial asset. When you consider your net worth, your business is the most significant line item on paper; in fact, according to most financial planners, it's like 80 to 90% of your net worth. But that wealth is without any value if it is not transferable. So is that net worth number even real?

Business value is not liquid. For this reason, it is very much misunderstood. Its value is not cash in the bank, a tradable security, or a certificate. Its value is not something that you can readily get your hands on. At least with some of your other investments, like real estate, you have something tangible. Real estate can't readily be liquidated, either; however, it's much more saleable than a business.

Like many owners, I expect your business probably produces a pretty good income for you and your family today. You may have possibly accumulated some wealth outside the business, too. Perhaps you have retirement investments, commercial real estate, an additional home, and some cash to play with. But all of that is peanuts compared to the value of your business.

What if I told you the Value Acceleration Methodology can *increase your net worth by a factor of five?* Does that get your attention? Well, yeah, that's a no-brainer. And the good news is, that *is* what I'm telling you and that is exactly what Value Acceleration can do. Now what if I followed up with telling you it will take a commitment to change, a new focus and execution, your energy and time, and will require you to challenge yourself to evolve your management system style to achieve increased net worth results? Would you be willing to change to achieve it?

Frankly, if your answer is no, I can't help you and neither can this book. You have already flushed your money buying this book and reading it will honestly be a waste of your time. But if you do care, and are willing to consider change, to increase your business to a level of value that gives you the opportunity to harvest your wealth, I want to help you make that happen. Read on.

What do you need your business to do in the future?
- Do you have a system that continuously focuses your team on maximizing the value of your business?
- Will cashing in (or failing to cash in) this asset affect your lifestyle at some point?
- Do you need the business to remain profitable after you leave it?
- Can the business run without you?

America alone sits on a stockpile of privately held business wealth, over $10 trillion. It is the greatest transfer of wealth in the history of mankind, set to hit in the next 10 to 20 years. Are you doing what you need to do today to identify, protect, build, harvest, and manage that wealth so the business successfully moves to the next stage in its life cycle? I can't answer that for you, but I can tell you that based on owner readiness research performed throughout the United States, the answer is no. Which means we are failing.

You aren't alone. There are nearly 28 million privately held businesses in the United States today. While most of those are holding companies with no payroll, roughly six million are operating companies. Those six million represent approximately $30 trillion in sales. Let's assume an average valuation of 50%, and these businesses represent approximately $15 trillion in privately held (mostly family-owned) wealth.

Exhibit A: Privately Held Businesses in the United States

	Sales Range	# of COS (thousands)	%	Sales $ (trillions)	%
Micro Market	<$5M	5,678	93.9%	3.57	12%
Lower Middle Market	$5M-$100M	351	5.8%	5.84	20%
Upper Mid Mkt & Above	>$100M	21	0.3%	20.33	68%
Total Employer Firms		**6,050**	**100%**	**29.74**	**100%**
Non-Employer Firms		21,708		0.99	
Total All Firms		27,758		30.73	

Source: Corporate Value Metrics, LLC 2013

Obviously, these businesses are not alike or equitably distributed. As you can see in Exhibit A, most of these businesses do $5 million or less in sales. These are considered "Micro Market" businesses, and there are approximately 5.7 million of them. To sum up, the micro market represents about 94% of the total privately held businesses in the market, $3.6 trillion in sales, and $1.8 trillion in value.

The "Lower Middle Market," which is defined as businesses with sales between $5 million and $100 million, represents 5.8% of the market. Collectively, they do about $5.8 trillion in sales and have a value of around $2.9 trillion. The "Upper Middle Market" has only 21,000 businesses and 0.3% of the market, but sales over $100 million. Although they only represent a fraction of the count-for-count market, they collectively hold the majority of sales with over $20 trillion and $10 trillion in value.

Now let's add the generation layer to our sample. Baby Boomers born between 1946 and 1964, nearly 80 million strong, own two-thirds of these privately held businesses. Today, the youngest Boomer is 52 years old and the oldest is 70... with the average Boomer at 61. Jump ahead 10 years: that average age moves from 61 to 71, the lower end moving to 62 and the oldest celebrating their 80th birthday. And as you might imagine (or maybe even know), it's *much* different moving from 60 to 70 than from 50 to 60. And the projection is, and rightly so, that a significant portion of these Boomer-owned businesses will transition during that time period. The *State of Owner Readiness Survey,* released by the Exit Planning Institute (EPI) and its partners, surveyed American privately held business owners of all sizes to benchmark the overall readiness of regional and national markets. In the survey, EPI reported that 76% of the business owners indicated they would like to transition in the next 10 years, while 48% indicated they would like to transition in the next five years. Do you see the problem? Do the math.

The trouble with that reality is that only two out of 10 businesses that go on the market will actually sell. A full 80% will not. Of those that sell, many will receive a lower multiple or sale price due to factors that include poor or nontransferable intangible assets. Just like a buyer's market in real estate, the private capital market will swing in favor of those acquiring versus those selling, and only the most attractive and ready businesses will move into the next stage of their life cycle. Take a moment and think about how you answered those questions regarding what you need your business to do in the future. And then ask yourself this: Can I afford to be one of the 80% that will not sell?

If you think you are immune because you are going to do a family transition instead of selling outside, you are not. Historical data shows that family businesses only have a 30% success rate through the second generation, 12% to the third generation, and 3% to the fourth and beyond (Family Firm Institute). You aren't in a better position because you have someone lined up to inherit your business. In many ways (that we will cover later), you are in a more complicated position. So again, ask yourself: Do I want my business to survive to my next generation? If I'm speaking from my heart as a parent, the answer isn't just yes. My answer is *of course*. My business is the legacy I'm building for my children, my grandchildren, and generations to come.

In fairness, the private capital market has been in the favor of the seller for some time now. And who knows? It very well could stay that way for a few years to come. But knowing what you now know about the realities in play and what you need from your business liquidation, is it wise to ignore the exit planning phenomenon?

In the professional services world, we have been hearing about this for 10 years. However, because Baby Boomers have turned 65 and have not retired, some feel that perhaps the tidal wave of exits is unlikely. Now, I don't want to sound harsh, but businesses are not the only thing that have a life cycle. People do too.

That said, many heavy-hitting advisors have been predicting the mass exodus for 10 years, and yes, in my opinion, the previous predictions were simply ahead of their time. They misunderstood the psychographics of Baby Boomers. The research shows that in contrast to the Traditionalists and Gen-Xers, Boomers value youth and success so strongly that they are the *least likely* to retire at the "standard" age of 65.

On top of that, the financial crash of 2007 and 2008 certainly put many owners' retirement plans on hold. No hardworking entrepreneur wants to go out in a recession and lose the majority of their net worth. Then, after the recession, outlooks improved, yet Boomers still did not want to exit. Why would they? Things were good again! And that aside, retirement and transition started to force owners to think critically about how unprepared they actually were for their third act, asking themselves,

"What would I even do?"

"Where would I invest the money if I did?"

And worse yet, "I can't live without the income from my business."

Studies have shown that business owners like you do actually struggle with the exit of their business for a variety of reasons, and that 75% of those who exit "profoundly regret" the decision within 12 months of exiting (Price Waterhouse). How can you change your paradigm and become part of the 25% who find fulfillment in their post-business future?

FACING THE REALITIES OF CHANGE

The times are changing, my friends. As I eluded to above, there are two significant strategic drivers at work today that, when viewed together, are going to influence the direction and decisions of Baby Boomer business owners over the next 10 years. And as we will see, the direction the Boomers take will massively influence the social and economic health of the market during that period.

First, you can't win the fight against Mother Nature and Father Time. You might outrun them in the short term, but aging is a part of living. As LeBron James, one of the greatest basketball players of all time, has said, "Father Time is undefeated." Ten years ago, the youngest Baby Boomer was 52… 52 is still young. Now you look in the mirror, as the average Boomer goes from 61 years old to 71, that is just a fact of life. In my experience (both professionally and personally), owners don't really start thinking about transition and retirement until they reach around age 55 because their work has been one of the most significant parts of their life, if not the biggest. However, as 80 million people age over the next 10 years, it is inevitable that Baby Boomer business owners' personal outlooks, health, and values will change out of necessity, if nothing else.

Second, we all know that what goes up must come down. The private capital market is no exception. From its inception, this has been an ongoing cycle. Positively, there has been an upside cycle since the last recession. We have seen unprecedented valuations and it has remained a seller's market. But there is unrest in the wind with specific eyes on the private capital market. A recent report commented "...fundamental industry shifts are impacting Middle Market companies today (Pitchbook, 2015)."

What impact do you think this will have on the market when all these business transitions begin to flow? Are market values likely to go up or down? Multiples are likely to fall. Only the best businesses will have the option to sell. Even if you choose an inside option (family, employees, partners, management), valuations may fall, leaving you at risk of receiving a lower payout. Financing will become more difficult—interest rates are likely going up. Does anyone disagree with that? Based on the market information available today, this is the most likely scenario over the next 10 years.

In 2015, there were indications of a decline, including lower Business-to-Consumer (B2C) capital investment and lower deal flow in resource industries. On top of that, there was an overall middle market decline in the areas of total capital invested, multiples, total capital raised, and total exits. It is tough to forecast the future with any certainty, and admittedly, the lower middle market was more stable. But if historical data shows anything, it illustrates that change is the only constant.

The market will change from a power position for sellers to a stacked deck for buyers. We will see the aging Baby Boomers flooding the markets to get out of their companies while experiencing a downturn in the public and private capital markets. What can't be predicted, and what I certainly don't know, is if this will start two years or five years from now. But *you know* when you plan to exit your business, so you'd be wise to consider that your timeframe benchmark.

If we stay on our current path, what is the probability that Baby Boomer business owners will be able to harvest the wealth they've spent their lives building? The answer: not good. Historical successful transition rates are between 20 and 30%. That means 70 to 80% of the possible wealth will not transfer, and at least $7 to $8 trillion will go unmonetized. The economic implications are enormous. But it is much more than just economic. The social impact could be devastating.

WHAT DOES "READINESS" MEAN?

In 2013, I was the local president of the EPI Northeast Ohio Chapter, and our group was approached to develop a value growth curriculum for business owners in the Greater Cleveland area. The first step was to understand our audience so we could tailor our messaging to be relevant to the needs of the owner. But I was shocked to find very little recent data available. How was I supposed to create a useful program when I didn't know anything about my students? And past that, how can we, as a community, align ourselves to support the needs of the business owners if we don't know what those needs are?

So powered by EPI and its partners, the inaugural *State of Owner Readiness Survey* was created to gauge the level of exit preparedness. The results were staggering.

Exhibit B: 2013 EPI State of Owner Readiness Survey Results Snapshot
- Two-thirds of owners are not familiar with all exit options
- 78% have no formal transition team; 83% have no written transition plan; 49% have done no planning at all
- 93% have no formal life-after-business plan
- 40% have no plans in place to cover illness, death, or forced exit

Exhibit B (Continued)
- Half of all owners need the company to remain profitable during and after the transition plan, yet 86% have not taken on a strategic review or a value enhancement project
- 56% felt they had a good idea of what their business is worth, yet only 18% have had a formal valuation in the last two years

It was honestly discouraging to see those numbers, especially in the community I have grown up in and love. With stats like that, is it any wonder owners are not able to transition successfully most of the time? Really?

I'm not trying to embellish or be an alarmist, but ding! Wake up! Owners are woefully unprepared. Based on this data, it doesn't take a rocket scientist to understand why. You are significantly underestimating what it takes to do "exit" well. Not to mention you don't recognize what exit means! Exit doesn't have to be an end-all, be-all. You could sell outright. You could stay in the business and just take chips off the table. Exit can be what you want if you plan for it. And if we, the business owners of today, don't change something, we're risking $8 trillion of family wealth and the potential to suffer the worst social crisis of modern times. And this isn't just happening in the United States. Baby Boomers, the most entrepreneurial generation to date, reside all over the globe.

But hey, let's go positive and think of the glass as half full. What if you were to improve transition rates? What impact could an injection of $8 trillion mean to our economy? How much good could you do with this unlocked wealth? What if you were able to harvest that wealth and put it to work in our economy and, in turn, empower the next generation of business owners?

Times are a-changin', my friends. And at this point, it's anyone's future. It's up to you to change them for the better. When it comes to harvesting business wealth, what's good for the goose is *definitely* good for the gander.

CHAPTER TWO

The Baby Boomer Business Owner

Baby Boomers have dominated our social and economic value systems since they burst onto the scene in 1946. The sheer size of this generation is enormous: nearly 80 million people. Odds are, you are a Baby Boomer. I definitely am. Regardless, Boomers are our largest and, in many ways, most influential population. How would you define the unique characteristics of the Baby Boomer generation and why is this relevant to the current business market?

Exhibit C: WMFC Generational Differences Chart Excerpt

	Traditionalists	Baby Boomers	Generation X	Millennials
Birth Years	1900–1945	1946–1964	1965–1980	1981–2000
Gen Nicknames	Moral Authority	"Me" Generation	Gen X	Gen Y; Echo Boomers
Key Attribute	Committed to Company	Ability to Handle Crisis	Work/Life Balance	Ambitious but Not Focused
Work Ethic	Pay Your Dues	60-Hour Work Week	Work Smarter, Not Harder	What's Next?
Views on Money	Pay Cash	Buy Now, Pay Later	Save, Save, Save	Earn to Spend
Core Value	Family/Community	Success	Time	Individuality

For one, Boomers grew up as a crisis generation, witnessing the impacts of the Civil Rights movement, the Vietnam War, the sexual revolution, the Cold War, and space travel. We lived through the building of America in the Fifties, including roads, interstates, bridges, and the move from cities to suburbs. Meanwhile, our Traditionalist parents, the "forgotten" generation who experienced hard times as children and prosperity later in life, preached "the American Dream" and instilled the spirit of reinvention and optimism into their bright-eyed, post-war children. Boomer children were special (and we were made to feel so) with a deep-seated ambition and a strong sense of work ethic. And apparently, this upbringing was the perfect formula for grooming 80 million kids to become real-world entrepreneurs. To this day, I'm not sure that my dad knew what he was doing when he ingrained these values into me and my siblings. It's likely he simply wanted to empower us to work hard and take risks since he watched his folks struggle through the Great Depression, but what an incredible parenting business model. We, Baby Boomers, entered adulthood hungry, and in turn, propelled our market forward with a laser focus on the ultimate goal: *success*.

Blues for Yesterday
Charlie Musselwhite

Rollin' down the highway
Rollin' into the settin' sun
It's a long long road
And I've had a good run
I got the blues for yesterday
Times was tough but we had fun

In contrast to Traditionalists who viewed it as a "dream" and Generation X who considered it as a way to get "there," Boomers considered education a birthright. As a result, we are well-educated, many having graduated from university with advanced degrees. However, there were more "qualified" candidates and not enough jobs for all of us as our group started to graduate—so naturally, those without traditional employment found other solutions using their knowledge and natural skills. They started businesses. Boomers are, after all, the most entrepreneurial generation in history (although I do think the Millennials will eventually outdo us here). So with that idealism and competence in hand, one out of every three Boomers created a business. Even today, Baby Boomers are twice as likely to launch a new business as Millennials (Kaufmann Foundation, State of Entrepreneurship Study, 2015). That's high, though not a surprising statistic, as we are risk-takers by nature, and are not afraid to continually reinvent ourselves.

I am a Baby Boomer and have reinvented myself several times, as I am sure you have too. I started my career as an auditor, then moved into supply chain logistics, then into information technology, and so on. The only constant in the first 24 years of my career was working for someone else, endorsing the back of the paycheck instead of signing the front. Now I have successfully transitioned from key man to small business owner and exit planner, which has been an incredibly fulfilling reinvention. As I'm sure it has for the 80 million others like me.

The Baby Boomer lives for now, and that applies to our views on money, which are very different from those of our parents. My father, who fought in World War II and grew up during the Great Depression, has established wealth and success, and yet he is still very conservative when it comes to spending. He drives a modest American car. He lives in the same standard suburban house he built in 1958. He can afford many luxuries in life, but he's a Traditionalist; that's not how he grew up. He mitigates risk, plays it safe, has modest expectations, and achieves satisfactory results.

Boomers spend. We want to live in nice houses, usually much bigger than our parents ever thought necessary. We drive the nicest car we can afford. We are not afraid to take on and live with debt. Though many Boomers have underfunded retirement, we take nice vacations. We embody and believe in the American Dream and when we want something or we want more, we find a way to get it. Even something as simple as televisions. Boomers have more than one TV. I have five. My dad has two. And because we overwhelmed society in business and sheer volume, our economic structure adapted to accommodate the Boomers' "Buy Now, Pay Later" mentality and behaviors.

REINVENTING THE RULES EVERY TEN YEARS

Demographers have likened the Boomer social effect to a pig moving through a python. At each stage of life, Baby Boomers' needs and desires have dominated business and culture. In the Fifties, birth rates drove the need for hospitals, diapers, baby food, homes, schools, teachers, textbooks, and toys including the Hula Hoop, Slinkys, and Frisbees. Remember those? Kids' television programming became a thing and shows like *The Mouseketeers, The Little Rascals,* and *Captain Kangaroo,* popped up on our television screens.

The Sixties drove the need for high schools and colleges. Between 1950 and 1975, the high school population doubled. And these "kids" were mobile with some spending power. They needed cars to get around. They went to movies, purchased soft drinks, and bought records by the Beatles and rock-and-roll artists. There was an unprecedented amount of money spent on cosmetics and toiletries. Now throw cheeseburgers in the mix; fast food franchises grew at a rate of 20% a year as we ate at McDonald's and other fast food establishments. And as we grew and found some success, we questioned the establishment. Boomers were rebellious and challenged the norm, starting with our conservative parents, which drove social unrest and resulted in change.

The Seventies saw Boomers move through college and navigate young adulthood concerns about lifestyle, personal identity, and self-esteem, and during that edification, the purpose of work became more important. A career was not "just a job" or an obligation; it was an adventure. Personal growth itself became an industry.

In the 1980s and 1990s, we shifted focus to careers and supporting our families, and so, boom! The home industry flourished. And in the midst of this era, the home experience was about to undergo the next major innovation. Boomers changed the world through the introduction of computers, mobile phones, and the Internet. Publications such as the *Wall Street Journal, Forbes,* and *GQ* had record growth. Another notable area of growth was the divorce rate. Boomers recorded the highest divorce rates and second marriages in history, bringing a new layer to the socioeconomic outlook and needs of the market. Daycare centers became important as Baby Boomer women entered the workforce with vigor and equal opportunities became a core value. The Boomers turned from hippies to yuppies and embraced their inner consumer, driving the Nineties to be one of the best decades ever financially.

In the early 2000s, we faced the dot-com crash, the housing bubble, 9/11, and financial crises. Consequently, we moved into the political arena. Today, Boomers are driving health care reform, long-term care, retirement planning, retirement housing, and social and national security reforms. True to their youthful spirit, willingness to challenge norms, and predisposition for reinvention, aging Baby Boomers are reshaping and redefining what retirement means.

So what's next for the Boomers and, accordingly, society? We will undoubtedly reshape and redefine every social and economic factor as we navigate our next 10 years. And like you and me, Baby Boomers who own businesses, who account for two-thirds of the privately held businesses in the market, are sitting on enormous (albeit trapped) wealth that we spent a lifetime building. What we do in the next decade to unlock that value and harvest that wealth will be the next, and potentially most keenly felt, transition in our lives and in the social and economic history of our country.

LONELY AT THE TOP: UNDERSTANDING THE MIND OF THE OWNER

Even with all of the generational information and statistics available today, business owners are misunderstood. And it's lonely at the top. You recognize it, and many who work with you see you as a uniquely different breed that can be very difficult to understand and navigate. You are a fighter and are used to (and comfortable with) going it alone if you have to. You want to surround yourself with others who can contribute to success and you build a team of talented people, but in the end, you are the one with skin in the game. You have to make the hard choices. You make the sacrifices. You live with the rewards and consequences of trusting others to care like you do. But you don't get to clock out and leave work at work. You built it, you feel it, you live it: *you are an entrepreneur*. That's what you do.

But looking forward to the future, it is abundantly clear that you need to instill that "owner-thinking" into the next generation of management in order to see your business into its next stage. It's a bad bet to go it alone or allow another year to go by with you as a critical, irreplaceable piece of the operations puzzle. You need successors that you have confidence in, a management team that feels the impact of their leadership, and an alignment with your vision for your family's future. Obviously, this is not a simple task.

Most business owners have a blend of left-brain and right-brain thinking, what Warren Bennis calls "whole brain" thinking. Left-brain thinking is logical, analytical, technical, controlled, conservative, and administrative. Right-brain thinking is more intuitive, conceptual, synthesizing, and artistic.

Entrepreneurs have more right-brain tendencies. Business owners are entrepreneurs who are creative, innovative, expressive, passionate risk-takers. However, as you've likely experienced throughout your career, the larger workplace employee mix tends to be the left-brain thinkers. This can make it challenging to stumble across the right people for your strategic or management team. I loved how Bennis put it in his book, *Managing the Dream:*

> *"One of the reasons so few corporate executives have successfully made the leap from capable manager to successful leader is that the corporate culture, along with society as a whole, recognizes and rewards left-brain accomplishments and tends to discount right-brain achievement."*

Most employees do tend to be more left-brain focused, looking for and following instructions rather than challenging the norm, taking chances, and being creative. Having been on both sides of this equation, first as an employee with the mind of an entrepreneur and later a business owner with the perspective of the staff, I appreciate the differences. Many employees, even incredible ones, have a hard time understanding the person they work for and follow.

One key difference is that the entrepreneurial business owner wears a different lens than the standard left-brain employee. For example, you could pull in your team to look over a list of action items written across a whiteboard, outlining a huge project or key initiative for your business. What do you see? Opportunity. What do they see? Tasks. That's not to say that your team can't crank through some tasks to amazing results. With your leadership and vision, they absolutely can. But what will happen when you choose to leave your business, explore the next act of your life, and empower your taskmasters to fill your shoes? Unfortunately, the vision leaves with you. The real accomplishment would be to challenge those like you, who exist in the whole brain space, to look at that same list and consider what they are building versus what they are doing. Just like you.

Being an owner is a tough job. A business owner has three roles: Management, Family, and Owner/Investor. First, as manager, you are clearly responsible for managing the business, and are often the best employee in the business. Second, and regardless of whether family is in the business, the business itself is the lifeblood for the family. When you get to third and fourth generation businesses, family ownership interests are typically vast. Some of the family actually work in the business, with

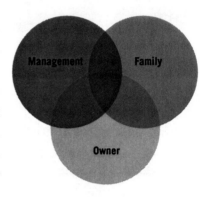

relationships involving brothers and sisters, fathers and mothers, sons and daughters, aunts and uncles. Often, even those who don't work in the family business think they should have a say in how it is operated. Third, the owner is an investor expecting, and *requiring,* a return on investment.

Every day, you are faced with decisions affecting all these constituents and roles, which are often in conflict. You always juggle what might be right for the business versus what may be best for the family.

> Several years ago, I met a friend for lunch at the Union Club in Cleveland. I could tell when he sat down there was something troubling him.
>
> So I asked him, "Hey, what's up?"

"Well, right after this lunch, I have to go back to the office and fire the president of my company."

And that's never a good day.

I listened to him and tried to offer some comfort and perspective, but it was really bothering him. We finished up our lunch and went on our separate ways, but his level of concern was troubling to me. So I called him up the next day to see how he was doing after the termination.

He told me that after our lunch, he returned to work and called the HR director and president to his office. He explained to the president that things were not working out. The president was missing his numbers and had lost the confidence of the staff. A change needed to be made. He told the president he was letting him go.

"How did he take it?" I asked.

"Honestly, not well."

He recounted how he had told the president to return to his office to clean out his stuff and leave that afternoon. A few hours later, my friend stepped into the excused president's office to see how the progress was coming and how he was doing. He walked in to see this man, the now former president, sitting in the chair across from his desk with his back to the door, head down and shoulders slumped over in disappointment. He went slowly up to the defeated ex-employee, put his hands on his shoulders, and said,

"Son, it's going to be okay. Your mom and I are here for you. We'll help you get through this."

That day, he had fired more than a non-performing president. He had fired his son.

Looking at my friend's story, the role of the owner can be painful, especially when family is involved. It was hard, but as the manager and investor in the business, he knew he had to do it. That didn't compensate for the anguish he felt, but he knew in the long run, this was the best thing for the business, his son, and the family—even if he was the only person who could see that. He knew his son would get back on his feet, but it wouldn't be at the family business.

STAKEHOLDERS IN YOUR SUCCESS

> *"...the business owner is, in fact, the giver of life."*
> —Leon Danco

Many depend on your ability to transition successfully. Employees who work for your company are one obvious group that needs continuity, but look past that. Look at who you are in your community.

Communities and charities that depend on your contributions, suppliers, and customers—all impacted. Privately held and family-owned businesses are the primary supporters of philanthropy through gifts of time and money. You likely support private schools, colleges, and the communities in which you live and operate. You, as the business owner, are at the very heart of the community. If the business goes, the community will suffer—maybe not even survive.

Further, many small business owners represent distribution of goods and services throughout the entire country. Many large manufacturers distribute their products through dealers and distributors, which are often small family-owned businesses. What happens if 70 to 80% of them perish?

> Not long ago, Peter Christman introduced me to a CEO of one of these manufacturers. I asked him what he was doing, if anything, to ensure that the distributors in his network were going to be able to transition their businesses.
>
> Shrug. "Not really anything."
>
> He said they were aware that it could be an issue, but hadn't given it a ton of thought or put any programs together to address it.
>
> "How many distributors do you have?" I asked.
>
> "About 200," said the CEO.
>
> "Okay. How many of the owners of these distributors are Baby Boomers?"
>
> "Oh, well, I'm not really sure. Probably 60 or 70%, maybe even more. But I do know that many of our distributors have been around a long time."
>
> "Did you know that Baby Boomers own about two-thirds of all privately held businesses? And if your distributors fall in line with the national averages, that means that roughly 120 of your distributors are Baby Boomers."

"Yeah. That sounds about right," said the CEO.

"Did you know in a recent survey conducted by the Exit Planning Institute, 76% of the owners surveyed, most of whom were Baby Boomers, indicated they would like to transition in the next 10 years? And are you aware that success rates on both inside and outside transitions are only about 20 to 30%?"

"No." I started to see his discomfort as he ran the numbers in his head.

"Yes, well those are the stats. And if we apply those stats to your distributors, that means that 75% of your Boomer distributors are likely to transition in the next 10 years—that's almost 50% of your distribution network, right?"

"Yes."

"With success rates of only 20 to 30%, about 20 to 40 of your distributors will be successful. The rest, somewhere between 80 and 100 of them, will fail to exit and remain operable so they'll shut down."

Silence. He now looked worried.

I looked him straight in the eye and asked, "What impact do you think losing 30 to 40% of your dealer network in the next 10 years will have on your business?"

"It would be devastating, frankly."

"Well, what are you doing about it?"

Now looking *me* straight in the eye, he replied, "What did you have in mind?"

Soon after that meeting, I spoke at the company's national conference to begin creating awareness and implementing the educational process. Then Peter and I went on to put together a multi-day exit planning and value acceleration workshop, sponsored and held at the manufacturer's headquarters. After the keynote, the CEO got up and announced the workshop date and described its purpose. "Your spouses and children are welcomed and encouraged to attend with you," the CEO suggested. Rather than wait and gamble on the tidal wave of exits, this CEO realized his professional ecosystem needed him to take a leadership role and get these processes underway on behalf of his distributors.

> *"When the distributor ceases to do business in this market area, the companies he represents are also out of business in that community." —Leon Danco*

This situation is common all over our great country. Small businesses, dealers, and distributors, are vital suppliers of goods and services throughout our supply chains. Big corporations' supply side is also affected. Many middle market, privately held businesses are suppliers to these big corporations.

If you are a corporate CEO or director of purchasing, ask yourself: what am I doing to ensure the continuity of my supplier base, many of whom are privately held businesses unprepared and unlikely to transition successfully?

CHAPTER THREE

Every Hero Has a Flaw

Business owners are heroes. You are leaders in your communities, distributors of many national products and services, and suppliers to many of our public corporations. Yet every hero has a flaw. And when it comes to your business, what's yours? Most likely, you aren't planning for the day you leave your business.

Why not? It seems like common sense that you should be paying significant attention to managing your most important financial asset. One reason is that most didn't begin with the end in mind. Most of you started, bought, or assumed a business for income, freedom, or a sense of duty toward the continuity of the family business. You've been successful, sure, but why stop there? Why not take that next step to create value, which is worth five times the income you generate? That reality is the exact problem that exit planning and value acceleration address. It is the method used to benchmark your business today, make meaningful adjustments,

---

The Pride

The Isley Brothers

What makes you want to do the best you can?

What makes you a better man?

What makes you try again before too long?

What keeps you standing strong?

What makes you say the things you want to say?

To make it a better day?

It's the pride that makes you feel that you belong

It's the pride that keeps you strong

---

and rapidly grow value so that you can monetize the value of your business when you are ready. If that's what it means to plan for exit, why don't more owners do exit planning? It seems like common sense, doesn't it?

> "At some point, the business owner must recognize that success has radically changed his relationship to his company. He must understand that businesses which survive do so because the founder has taken measures to assure the continuity of his company. The business owner must change his role from that of super-employee to that of respected leader and teacher, who must gain his ultimate glory in the accomplishments of those who follow him." —Leon Danco

Based on our nature alone, there are predispositions at play that make Baby Boomer owners hesitant to approach exit planning. The idea of leaving your business works against the core value embedded in each of us. Why would I choose to leave behind my successful career and my youth? It is not an easy pill to swallow. And honestly, many (myself included) don't want to stop working. I love my business. But if we're honest with ourselves, there are other reasons at play. Ask yourself these questions:

- Are you afraid of the future? Do you fear getting older?
- Do you need the income from the business to support your lifestyle?
- Do you know what you are going to do once you leave your business?
- Are you worried about word getting out about your plans to exit?
- Are you misinformed about what exit planning is?
- Do you find exit planning confusing and complicated?
- Do you see the clear benefit to exit planning?

- Do you consider exit planning important, but not urgent?

There are many reasons owners don't do exit planning, but when you break it down, it seems to circle around a few central areas of discomfort.

BABY BOOMERS ARE AFRAID OF GETTING OLD

Why does fear come into the equation for a generation so adaptable and comfortable with change? Baby Boomers don't want to grow old. You don't want to become irrelevant. And most of you don't want to "exit." You have spent your lifetime navigating crisis, embracing reinvention (far beyond the capacity of your parents and even your children), and with that, you have accomplished incredible things. You are successful. It's no wonder that you would have a gut reaction to the word "exit." Exit sounds like the end.

In today's paradigm, "exit" is a disconcerting word. I have been advised by some of my closest advisors and partners that I should change the name of my company, the Exit Planning Institute, to strike the "e-word" altogether. Many of my own clients, who are predominantly professional exit planning advisors, believe that they should not even use the word "exit" when talking about exit planning with business owners. "We should use a softer word like 'transition' or 'succession,'" they say, "because owners are intimidated by the word 'exit'." Hmmm.

The truth is these advisors aren't wrong. Discussing exit does prompt a negative reaction nine times out of 10. But what's really going on here? You may be intimidated, but not by the word. The fact is that exit planning evokes fear and negative emotions only because of the way you view it, your paradigm. Changing the word used to define the process won't change the feelings that word evokes.

I'm a Baby Boomer too, and I have challenged myself to never shy away from that word. Rather, I see this as an opportunity to truly connect with my peers, in this case you, to address those fears and redefine the paradigm that villainizes exit planning. I find that exit is only negatively perceived by owners who perceive the word to represent "the end." The end of your youth, which makes you feel like your best days are behind you. The end of your career, which makes you feel like your success is ending too. The end of your life, which also means your last and final separation from all the people and things that you've loved. "The end" evokes these feelings of separation and it doesn't feel good. Talking about your exit makes you feel old.

Why are we so afraid of getting old? Reaching the third act of our lives should be a celebration. If you have planned accordingly, your third act could actually be your best act. That's not to say growing up, being in my teens, meeting my future wife, and my college years weren't great. That was my first act and it laid my foundation. And then my second act, the days of having a family, building my career, and raising my children, was undeniably wonderful. I wouldn't change them for anything.

Now as I get older and approach the days of my third act, times are just as exciting. Just different. And in a lot of ways, *better*. I have more disposable income than before, so I travel more and I drive a nicer car. I don't have to worry about my children as much as I used to, as they are on their own paths now. And in turn, I have gotten to know my bride of 34 years again.

I had this fear that I would have an abundant amount of free time if I distanced myself from being in the business 60 hours a week, but I was wrong. I certainly don't have more free time. If you speak to my wife and children, they will tell you they have never seen me busier. I'm just busy with the things I want to do instead of what I have to do.

My friend and mentor, Pete Christman, is known to many as the "original exit planner." When Pete speaks on the subject of third act planning, he has a simple exercise he likes to do with the group. Give this a try:

Write down the age of the person who has lived the longest in your family.

Now write down your age.

Calculate the difference.

Is that number between 20 and 40 years? If so…now is your third act.

If you exit your business at 60 or even 70, it's likely you will live another 20 to 30 years. And what is important is having a vision for what you are going to do with that time. You fear becoming obsolete, so what are you doing to stay relevant? What are you going to do with your time? Wallow in pity, wishing you still had your business to keep you busy? After all the positive things you have experienced in your life and brought to the world? Your third act won't be dismal if you continue to pursue life with the vigor and enthusiasm of your younger days. Take care of yourself and your health so you can experience your third act to the level that you deserve. And pass on your wealth and wisdom to secure your family's future.

BUSINESS OWNERS ARE TRAPPED

Many owners are trapped in their businesses, unable to unlock their wealth, because they are so reliant on the income the business brings and are financially unprepared for life without that income. Let's face it. Income is one of the many perks of business ownership. You live well. You live in a nice home in a nice neighborhood. Your children have the opportunity to attend private schools. You sit in the best seats at the ballgame or concert hall. You drive a nice car. You have country club memberships and possibly a second home on the lake or at the beach. You have become a pillar in your community. Plus, once your business is established and your kids have moved out, you have more disposable income.

Some of you may feel some financial freedom. You've arrived! And you really do deserve it. What it took for success in ownership was a lot of personal sacrifice. Your employees will never understand the risks, the missed paydays, the long hours, the times you chose work over family, and the worry and grief that comes with business ownership. You have more than earned your income.

But you spend a lot too, right? And the fact is, you may not have adequate resources outside the business to support your lifestyle without that business income. Let's assume the average owner benefit of 10% of sales. If you sell your business for $2.5 million, you will clear around $1.75 million, after taxes and fees. Let's say you invest that entire amount in a reasonably safe retirement portfolio and earn 6% before taxes. What's your new income? Your annual income just went from $500,000 to $105,000 per year. So you've worked hard your entire life, and in your last act, you take a $400,000 pay cut? Ouch.

So it is easy to see that if you haven't planned properly, you are now trapped. You need the income from the business to support your lifestyle. Even if you pull cash out of the business in your later years to invest in retirement, you face the risk of undercapitalizing the business. So what do you do?

Sean Hutchinson, a close friend and industry leader in value acceleration, will not work with an owner who does not have a "growth mindset," meaning a commitment and passion for building a strong company with high-growth goals. This is because of a common phenomenon: when an owner realizes later in life that he has not planned properly financially, he tries to catch up by sucking resources out of the business or transitions it to the children, but still pulls a salary even though he is not there anymore. And if the business is not growing, that owner is actually decapitalizing the overall value and weakening the probability of the business's perpetuity after he leaves. Not to mention, you will pay the price for that kind of misguided strategy at the time of sale. If you decide to try and sell that business, you will likely receive a below-average, discounted offer (if you receive an offer at all on this weakened enterprise). Or the terms of the offer will require you to financially assume the risks of the buyer. Or you might say, never mind, these buyers aren't paying what I need. I'll just hand it over to my daughter. And in that family transition situation, you pass off an undercapitalized business as a gift to the next generation, making it even tougher for her to succeed. So why does Sean insist you have a "growth mindset" before he comes on board with your business? Because growth is key to unlocking the income trap that keeps you stuck in your business.

BUSINESS OWNERS DON'T KNOW WHAT TO DO NEXT

I was talking with a retired accountant about recent exit planning trends and got onto the subject of why owners don't like to think about leaving their businesses. He got an indignant look on his face that stopped me.

"Are you kidding? It's not just owners, Chris. It's all of us."

"Sure, I agree, but it's a little different for owners," I said, surprised I had hit a sensitive spot.

"Maybe the financial risk is different, but the feeling is the same. I retired and my wife and I moved down to Florida, just like we'd planned. I'm out on the golf course the other day and a guy walks up to my foursome and says to me, 'So who were you when you were somebody?'"

Baby Boomers are the inventors of the 60-hour work week. We found passion and reward in our careers. And now, we all know someone, not unlike my accountant friend, who worked their entire life, retired as planned, and struggled to find real fulfillment. That fact has tarnished our perception of what life-after-business looks like. Even if you overcome fear and are financially prepared, most of us don't know what to do next. It doesn't help that most Boomer owners don't actually want to exit their businesses. You want to keep it as long as you can. It's not just the income; it's your identity. You are the business.

Life-after-business planning feels like a soft topic, and as a business owner, you have a lot of immediate demands that keep you from finding time to really explore that part of your future. And it isn't as simple as figuring out how much money you need to pack up the house, move to the beach, and play golf four times a week. As your future rapidly becomes your present, your lack of attention to this area is the source of your discomfort. Don't just hang it up. You owe it to yourself to plan a third act that sets you up to stay connected with your identity and excel in your new ventures, embracing who you've been and who you want to be... while staying relevant.

BUSINESS OWNERS DON'T WANT ANYONE TO KNOW THEY ARE PLANNING TO EXIT

Shhhh. Keep your voice down. I don't want anyone to know I am thinking of exiting. If word gets out, the employees will leave, the customers will leave, the suppliers will abandon me...are you kidding me?

> Several years ago, my partner and I met with the owner of a successful engineering firm. The owner was a 73-year-old, tough, hard-nosed kind of guy.

"Listen," he said, "I want to make this very clear. I don't want anyone to know I am considering exiting. The whole place, everything I built, will fall apart if they do."

"Really?" I said, looking surprised.

"Yeah, really—what do you mean?" he asked.

"Everyone already knows!" I said, "They are probably all wondering what you are doing and, frankly, are afraid because you are leaving them out of the loop! You are 73 years old, for Christ's sake!"

What do you think would be more appealing to your stakeholders? Being left in the dark wondering when the big news will come (with their most proactive option for survival being a contingency plan for the day your business doesn't exist anymore)? Or do you think they would find it more appealing to participate in a well thought-out succession plan that addresses the future and maps out an orderly transition?

When I meet with my executives, I make it a point to ask them, "Do you think doing that will make our business more attractive to a potential buyer?" or "Does that new client have any value if we were to sell in three years?" I have them fill out quarterly enterprise scorecards that ask them to rate the value of our intangible capital and provide an analysis. I want my leaders to know that building our business with high market value would be a major success regardless of the endgame. The result of knowing and participating in exit strategy has made my staff stronger leaders and better strategic thinkers. And I'd challenge you to be more willing to be transparent with the leaders you rely on to operate your business. You need to address this immediately so you can start to grow and benefit from the accomplishments of a staff that truly embodies ownership thinking.

BUSINESS OWNERS HAVE PRIORITIES THAT FEEL MORE URGENT THAN EXIT PLANNING

You, as the owner and operator, are often the best employee in your business. Your wisdom and experience are needed, particularly if you have not identified and groomed a successor. The daily success of the business is most likely still dependent on you. You may know that exit planning is something you need to do, but you are too busy solving the problems of today. Exit planning ticks further down your priority list and becomes something you plan to do down the road.

What you need to understand is that every day, you make decisions that impact your exit. You can address this by integrating the principles of exit planning and value acceleration into the daily operations of the business now. Exit strategy is business strategy. It's not a project to be taken on somewhere down the road. It integrates your personal, business, and financial goals and serves as a guide for success. When done correctly, exit planning provides immediate return and benefits on top of what is possible in the future. This is not the common perception of exit planning, since your current paradigm causes you to view it as something else.

Every month, I hold a workshop called the "Owner Roundtable," which brings together high net worth owners and entrepreneurs in the Greater Cleveland area to get educated on how to manage their business value. One of the coolest things about the Owner Roundtables is the collaboration between peers as they discuss their businesses. I observed an interesting exchange between three business owners who all agreed they did not want to exit and would prefer to keep their businesses: Hank (age 52), Chuck (age 61), and Mike (age 66). Hank, the youngest of the three, made the comment that he still felt young and vibrant.

> "I have no desire to exit," Hank said, "but I would like to set up my business so that if a buyer opportunity presented itself or something terrible happened, God forbid, I would be in a position to harvest that value. Honestly, thinking about disability and death impacting my business value scares the h*** out of me."

Chuck, who had recently turned 61, had a different point of view. Age had snuck up on him and now he was feeling it.

> "It wasn't until recently that I even thought about exiting," he said, "and I hate to admit it, but I'm literally feeling older. I'm getting worried about how long I can keep this up. My energy is not what it used to be and I need to sustain that energy level to operate my business. I'm not in a place where I can sell, even if I wanted to, because I haven't figured out how to get my money off the table."

The last owner, Mike, was in the midst of a family transition, bringing his children into the business. He was already a second-generation family owner, and in his eyes, the business had been on "autopilot" for quite some time. Mike thought that after his kids were up and running, he'd start to slow down.

> "I'm shocked: just the opposite happened. Having my kids in the business has brought me back to life. My energy has increased in the family business and I've been buying others, too. I've never been busier, or if I'm being honest, happier."

Exit planning is important and you'd be wise to make it a priority now. It only becomes urgent when you wait. Like the three owners above, you face new concerns, challenges, and opportunities as you approach your third act. Implementing value strategies into your business now will provide you with the independence, choices, and freedom to properly plan how to stay engaged and relevant.

BUSINESS OWNERS ARE MISINFORMED

> *66% of business owners have not completed any formal education related to transitioning their business.*
> —*EPI State of Owner Readiness Survey,* 2016

Most likely, you are not educated about how to exit your business, let alone what exit planning really is. Why would you be? For most of us, it is a once-in-a-lifetime event. You have no idea how challenging it is and how much the odds are against your successful transition. It's understandable. You don't know what you don't know. Exit planning is simply good business strategy, but few view it as such. This book is a step in the right direction. It's time to educate yourself and change your paradigm so you can change your outcome.

Part of the issue is that many of the advisors you rely on to teach and guide you through the exit planning process are misguiding you. Is exit planning estate planning? Is it tax planning? Is it financial planning? Does it mean selling the business? Or does it mean transitioning it to your children or your employees? Yes, yes, yes, yes, yes.

Exit planning is all of those things and more. Your advisors, most of whom are functional and technical, view exit planning from their point of view. Few advisors treat exit planning with the holistic view that I am teaching you in this book. They, too, focus on the end. And so does most of the literature about exit planning.

Much of your advisors' misinformation is understandable. Most of them also have functional myopia. Most have a particular expertise, be that financial planning or accounting or law, among many others. Such advisors tend to view the world of exit planning from this functional and technical perspective. On top of that, most advisors don't work well as a team. It complicates the process when your accountant, your attorney, your insurance agent, and your financial planner are giving you conflicting advice. Add your spouse's opinion to the equation, plus the cost of dealing with all these "plans," and you just write off everyone's advice as more trouble than it's worth. Who wants to deal with six different advisors with six different plans anyway? You don't want plans...you want action! You want results!

All of this makes exit planning sound complicated and time consuming. The fact is, exit planning *is* complicated and time consuming. In the past, we treated exit planning like a project rather than a way of operating. Not having a common framework which fits all the pieces together makes it more confusing. So rather than deal with it, the tendency is to put your head in the sand. But with Value Acceleration, we now have a common definition and common framework to bring exit planning into the present.

BUSINESS OWNERS DON'T WANT TO EXIT

The idea of the Owner Roundtable has spread in Northeast Ohio (and across the nation), so now I have a few different sessions going on all the time, and I use this as an opportunity to invite high-caliber advisors to sit in, and sometimes speak, so they can learn what it means to be an owner.

Two months ago, I posed a question to a group of Baby Boomers:

> *"Which of these sounds more appealing to you? Would you rather (a) liquate your business at some point in the future or (b) keep the business and have it produce an ongoing dividend without you having to be there every day?"*

What do you think the answers were?
What is your answer to that question?

It was unanimous.
Every single one of them answered (b). Keep the business.

Not one of them would exit their business if they didn't have to. The business represents more than your identity; for many, it is your life. The game of business is what you enjoy doing. Given a choice, you honestly wouldn't do anything else. You are already doing what you want to do.

The advisors in the room were stunned. Advisors who make up this industry (left-brainers by definition) have this perception that all owners want out. All the advice and messaging is about making a plan to get you out. But this perspective is wrong. And though these advisors' help is needed, it's unwanted because their message itself makes it clear that they don't actually understand you. If an advisor met with you and said, "Hey, let's make and adopt an exit plan that gives you options. You can keep the business and have more flexibility. You can sell the business at the highest multiple. We'll get you to a place where you have choices," would you be more receptive to the concept of exit planning? Obviously.

All of the owners said they knew the "number" they needed to exit and live comfortably, but given the choice, they would stay in. Moreover, they saw the business as the least risky asset in their portfolio. One owner pointed out the recent volatility in the market.

> *"Where would I even put my money if I got it out? I don't trust some third party to manage my asset. If I keep it in my business, I can manage my assets."*

He is not alone in thinking this. Most owners don't trust third parties to manage their assets. And as a business owner who has navigated crisis and established success, you believe you are the best steward of your money. In truth, if you did sell and put the money into a diversified, professionally managed portfolio, it would never produce the kind of income you produce in your business today.

There are plenty of reasons why you haven't started exit planning. Part of the reason is there is too much emphasis on the end. Instead, you should focus on what you can do right now to make your business and personal planning better. If you embrace that, you'll see major results and have lots of exit options, including sustaining your involvement in the business even longer (which is probably what you want). Get yourself in a position to harvest the value you have built. An investment in your exit is an investment in creating a better lifestyle right now *and* in the future. Now is the time to pull your head out of the sand.

CHAPTER FOUR

Changing Your Paradigm

Many successful businesses adopt a focused vision for who they are, who they serve, and what they are ultimately doing. I call it the organizing principle. It should be simple and easy to understand. Your staff should know it. This simple truth sits at the core of everything you do, from daily operations to strategic planning.

For my flagship company, the Exit Planning Institute (EPI), our organizing principle is "Change the Outcome." Every day, I challenge my team (and myself) to consider how the day's accomplishments changed the outcome for those we serve: Baby Boomer business owners. And as I've become more engaged and passionate about the work we do at EPI, it has become clear that exit planning is a misunderstood discipline. Despite the major gains and benefits you glean in value growth, exit planning has been underutilized by owners like you.

Centerfield
John Fogerty

Well, beat the drum and hold the phone
The sun came out today
We're born again, there's new grass on the field
A-roundin' third and headed for home
It's a brown-eyed handsome man
Anyone can understand the way I feel

Oh, put me in coach, I'm ready to play today
Put me in coach, I'm ready to play today
Look at me, I can be, Centerfield

A paradigm shift is needed. My belief is that with awareness and education, you change your perception of "the exit" itself. This one paradigm shift will change your fear of the exit to an embrace of the future. And as others like you change their mindsets, the new worldview of exit planning could improve the rate of businesses that successfully transition from two out of ten to eight out of ten. It could take the 75% dissatisfied with their post-life to 75% thriving and being happy in their third act. In the process of changing your paradigm, you have a real opportunity to own your destiny and change your outcome.

HOW DO YOU DEFINE EXIT PLANNING?

To redefine the paradigm of what exit planning is, we should start with a sense of what it has been. Let's look at some recent definitions of exit planning.

Richard Jackim, the co-author of *The $10 Trillion Opportunity* and co-founder of EPI, defines exit planning this way: An exit plan asks and answers all the business, personal, financial, legal, and tax questions involved in transitioning a privately owned business. This plan includes contingencies for illness, burnout, divorce, and death. Its purpose is to maximize the value of the business at the time of exit, minimize taxes, and ensure the owner is able to accomplish all his or her personal and financial goals in the process. There's no denying this is an accurate definition of what an exit plan addresses. But is exit planning a

Exhibit D

"plan?" **No.** Exit planning is not like a valuation report. You don't find success in exit planning by creating a printable document that captures the static nature of your business. Exit planning is dynamic. That said, Rich hits on some important points. Let's read on.

Peter Christman, the other co-founder of EPI and author of *The Master Plan,* has one of the best conceptual definitions of exit planning. It has become the basis for the core principles on which EPI's curriculum is built. According to Pete, exit planning is achieved through developing a business transition plan that addresses three things: (1) maximizing the value of your business, (2) ensuring you are personally and financially prepared, and (3) ensuring you have planned for the third act of your life. We refer to this concept as the "three legs of the stool."

Think about it. If you have a three-legged stool, what happens if each leg isn't equal? What if one leg is missing altogether? The point is, all three legs are equally important to success. Pete is absolutely right in emphasizing the importance of balance in exit planning. If you focus solely on business and financial factors (ignoring your personal needs), you are likely to be one of the 75% "dissatisfied" with their exit. Master Planning is an important concept (which we will explore more in Chapter 5), but here's the question: Is exit planning a "concept?" **No.** Exit planning is not an abstract idea or notion existing at 30,000 feet. Exit planning touches the ground.

Patrick Ungashick, the author of *Dance in the End Zone: The Business Owner's Exit Planning Playbook,* defines exit planning as "the conscious effort to grow your business in a manner that efficiently converts ownership into personal financial freedom and peace of mind." I like this definition because it plainly states the output exit planning provides: "freedom and peace of mind." That sounds good to me. You have spent years feeling the responsibility and sacrifice ownership requires (and you feel it 24 hours a day). You would be happy to convert that effort into some rest and relaxation in your third act. But again, I ask, is exit planning a "conscious effort?" **No.** It takes effort, but exit planning is not the effort itself.

John Brown, the founder of BEI and author of *How to Run Your Business So You Can Leave It In Style,* expands on the definitions I've outlined here by describing exit planning as "an established process that creates a written roadmap or Exit Plan, involving efforts of several professions facilitated and led by an exit planning advisor." John hits two big nails on the head. Exit planning, like any multi-step project, should involve a process, and it involves the overlap of several professions to achieve a well-rounded, methodical exit. So is exit planning a "process?" **No.** The collaboration of teams using a proven process is an absolute necessity in exit planning. But that alone is not exit planning.

SO WHAT IS EXIT PLANNING?

Exit planning is simply good business strategy. It is your value management system that makes the timing of your exit irrelevant. Exit planning is laser-focused on what you can do right now to grow the value of the business and drive income. Forget the future. Focus on today. By focusing your approach on building a business with characteristics that drive value and integrating your personal and financial objectives into it now, you will have lots of options to exit on your timeline and terms.

> *Exit planning combines the **plan, concept, effort,** and **process** into a clear, simple **strategy** to build a business that is transferable through strong human, structural, customer, and social capital. The future of you, your family, and your business are addressed by exit planning through creating value today.*

Exit planning is about building, harvesting, and preserving family wealth for generations to come. Ditch the current paradigm, and make the shift. You can evolve by integrating best-in-class business practices into your daily operations. The key is managing your enterprise value to drive positive outcomes, including a better lifestyle. A well-planned business succession program efficiently transfers business value to your personal legacy, while honoring the needs of your stakeholders and creating a developed vision for your third act.

Exit planning is easy to understand, but it will not necessarily be easy to accomplish. You have to be willing to change. Value acceleration actions require tireless commitment and relentless execution. It can be hard to go this path alone. Collaboration is your ally. Working as a team uncomplicates the process and improves your exit planning experience. You are at the center of the process, flanked by a seasoned multi-disciplinary team to support your success.

CHANGE YOUR PARADIGM

You know that successful business transition rates are very poor; 70 to 80% fail. But that also means that 20 to 30% succeed. Are there specific things that those owners did to set themselves up for a successful transition? What can you learn from their success? Do you have the motivation to emulate and repeat these success patterns?

Changing outcomes for business owners like you and your families starts with changing your point of view—*your paradigm*—about exit planning.

1. **Paradigm shift is required.** Exit planning is simply good business strategy integrated with your personal and financial goals and objectives.

2. **Business is personal.** Personal financial goals and personal aspirations should be driving the business, not the other way around. There will be times when you have conflicting value systems. Owning a business is personal.
3. **Value is the primary long-term goal**—not income. This sounds like a subtle play on words, but in reality, this is a significant paradigm shift.
4. **Focus on the present, not the future.** Much of what has been written about exit planning focuses on the endgame. But it isn't accomplished by focusing too far down the road. Your successful exit is based on what you do now; every day counts. There is no reason you can't benefit today and in the future. You can do both.

Exhibit E: Owner Paradigm Shift

From	>	To
"Exclusive" Point of View	>	"Inclusive" Point of View
Future	>	Present
Business	>	Personal, Financial, and Business
Income	>	Value
Owner	>	Stakeholders
Tangible Assets	>	Intangible Assets
Tax Number	>	Real Number
Project	>	Process
Plans	>	Action
Individuals	>	Team
VERSUS	>	AND

5. **Manage your five stages of value creation.** Value acceleration is achieved by focusing on the multiple, which is based on the strength of your intellectual capital (your intangible assets).
6. **Your intangible assets must be transferable.** Your business value can only be harvested if your intellectual capital can be passed to a buyer. You need to understand the difference between attractiveness and readiness.
7. **Adopt a process.** Great planning makes execution imperatives clear. There are sequential steps that should be respected to keep you moving in the right direction. Taking the time to get organized before you execute will help determine what you should be doing and in what order. It will ensure you are working on the right things.
8. **You must execute.** A plan helps you prioritize, organize, and focus. But without the will to execute, a plan will not create action. I would also argue that much of what is written focuses on what you should do. But "how" is a question that often remains unanswered. Value Acceleration is the way to execute and deliver.
9. **Measure your results.** You need a scorecard and a management system that measure and reinforce your focus on value growth. Your value management system needs to be flexible and should be frequently (and quickly) recalibrated. Metrics offer a systematic approach to accomplish this.
10. **Involve your team.** It takes a diverse team to be successful. You can't do it alone. And there are many stakeholders depending on your success.
11. **Invest in your success.** You will need to spend some money and time to be successful. Accept that. Back up your commitment with investments in creating value. Bringing in the necessary expertise will get you over the hump and keep you focused.

Investment in exit planning is justifiable with growth of enterprise value as the goal. It will pay dividends far exceeding the costs. Put it in your budget.

Your business is your most precious, and often your largest, financial asset by far. I could argue that it is likely much more than that. For many of us, it's the love of our life. Don't let it perish after you are gone. It's a seed that will be cherished and will bring happiness and prosperity to all those who follow you. Step up to that responsibility.

MAKING THE TIMING IRRELEVANT

Let's determine if there is a "right time" for you to exit. Look at the charts that follow. Bear in mind, my intention is not for these charts to be viewed or relied on from a technical standpoint. They simply illustrate an attempt to "time the market" as it relates to transitioning your business.

The first is a Personal Timing Chart that implies that as you age, your enthusiasm, passion, and energy levels start to decline. This decline begins around the age of 62.

Exhibit F: Personal Timing Chart

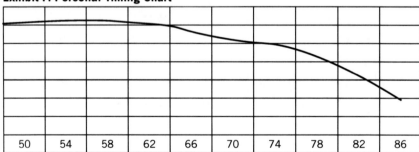

Next comes the Business Life Cycle Chart, just like you saw in Economics 101. Early in your business's life, it grew at a rapid pace. Eventually, that growth slows and flattens out. Then begins the slow decline. You can change the life cycle by introducing new products and services, expanding into new markets, and so on.

Exhibit G: Business Life Cycle Chart

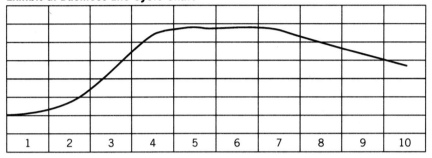

The Private Capital Market Timing Chart represents the up and down cycles of the private capital market.

Exhibit H: Private Capital Market Timing Chart

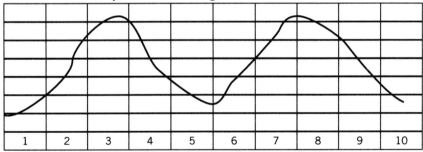

Look at the three charts. What age do you think would be best for you to exit? Maybe between 68 and 72 when you are tired and your business is in decline, but the market is on its way up? Or you might say between 72 and 76. You are at the peak of the second market cycle, plus you just rode that wave of growth right before the market declines. But wait, you'd be 76. Is that really better, given the circumstances, than you exiting at age 58 when your business is experiencing its greatest growth and the market is nearing its peak in the first cycle?

Let's be honest. How often does market timing really work? Rarely. Is there a right time to exit? **No.** There are good times and bad times presented by the private capital market. For example, when I wrote this book, it was one of the best times in history to maximize the value of your business by selling it to a strategic buyer, a private equity firm, or a family office. In fact, as I write, many industries are producing the highest multiple ever. But that doesn't mean it's the right time for you. And no timing predictions can prepare your business for the unplanned. You don't know when you are going to run out of gas. You might get hit with a health or family issue that takes your enthusiasm and passion for the business down rapidly. You might experience an unexpected interruption of your business that changes the course of its life cycle. You could lose or win a major customer. There could be a market innovation that marginalizes your core product or service. You could lose a key employee. Who knows? The point is that forecasting the private capital market is likely your *worst* strategy for harvesting your wealth.

Luck and predictions aside, it's nearly impossible for an unprepared owner to time the market. Do you want to rapidly grow your business value and unlock your personal wealth? Then you need to focus on building an attractive business now, because a good business will sell in good times or bad. Build value into your business every day through exit planning; evaluate your plans, personal and business; assess your ability to execute; and ask yourself every 90 days: Do I want to keep growing or do I want to sell? That you can control. And that will make your exit timing irrelevant.

SECTION TWO

Core Concepts of Value Acceleration

Now you will review the principles on which Value Acceleration is built, including the importance of aligning personal, financial, and business goals, and the concept of Master Planning. Look at the difference between focusing on value versus income. Review the Five Stages of Value Maturity and the importance of managing intellectual capital: the key to accelerating and harvesting value. Consider, not only why planning is critical, but why execution is even more important. Finally, explore the importance of vision, management team alignment, measurement, and rhythm.

CHAPTER FIVE

The Third Leg of the Stool

Personal, financial, and business goals must be in alignment in order for you to successfully grow and transition your business. The alignment of the three legs of the stool is a concept called Master Planning, created by Peter Christman, a very good friend and mentor to me and many others. Pete, or "The Original" as we affectionately call him, is the co-founder of EPI and was a very successful investment banker for Geneva Capital. As the leading sales guy for Geneva, he was selling many of his clients' businesses at a premium. But he noticed that despite having a lot of money after the sale, many of his clients were miserable. He realized that the cause of this was because all the personal planning was happening *after* the sale.

Shine On
Eric Bibb

I know what you've been through, I see
Keep on when your mind says quit
Dream on 'til you find your living it
Don't stop 'til you win your prize
Lean on all the love that is in my eyes
You're a diamond to me, yes you are
That's what you're born to do
Shine on

Pete realized he needed to change this. He partnered with Richard Jackim, the president of The Christman Group, Pete's investment banking firm at the time, and they began to study this phenomenon. They authored *The $10 Trillion Opportunity,* and founded EPI in 2005. In 2007, due to demand from professional advisors who wanted to learn how to perform more effective exit planning, Pete and Rich introduced the Certified Exit Planning Advisor (CEPA) credentialing program and began teaching that to have a successful exit, personal, financial, and business goals must all be in alignment.

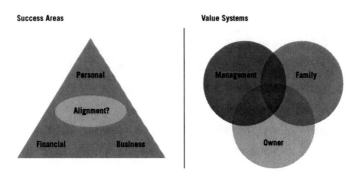

Exhibit I: Drivers and Influences

- Define success from several viewpoints
- Know your important relationships

SUCCESS AREAS OF A MASTER PLAN

Ten years passed before Pete introduced his new book, *The Master Plan*. This book was written with business owners in mind, and specifically discusses how to use Master Planning to align the three legs of the stool into one "Master Plan," putting the owner and the owner's family at the center of the process.

Review the value systems chart again. Your definition of "success" needs to be defined in each of these areas, and from several viewpoints, considering the important relationships that come from your roles of family member, manager, and owner.

From a personal standpoint, you need to consider things like family and friends, self-worth, self-identity, philanthropy, health, what you do for fun, and for many, your religion and personal spiritual values.

Financially, you need to consider your income requirements, risk profile, personal wealth, retirement needs, and long-term health.

And for your business, you need to consider things like the direction of the business, factors that drive value into the business, the salability and ongoing viability of the business, the predictability of the business's income stream, the overall health of the business, and your staff, systems, management succession, and business risks.

> *"...I don't believe your business is your life, though it does and can play a significantly important role in your life. But before you can determine what that role will be, you must ask yourself these questions: What do I value most? What kind of life do I want? What do I want my life to look like, to feel like? Who do I wish to be?"* —Michael Gerber, E-Myth

Value Acceleration is a management and life planning system focused on value *and* income; it integrates the three legs, putting you and your family at center of the process. It promotes team play for all stakeholders. It clarifies the roadmap to success. Accountability is built into the system. It has clear deliverables and benefits. And it is measurable. If Master Planning is the concept, Value Acceleration is how you implement it.

In addition, Value Acceleration can also be used as a development, intergenerational, and employee transition measurement tool, educating the next generation of management about factors that enhance value. It can be used as a tool to teach your team how to create value, not just more income; measure their performance; and benchmark value creation.

PLANNING YOUR BEST ACT

Pete's thought that your personal, financial, and business goals need to be aligned is correct. But which one would you say you give the least attention to today? Personal planning.

It's pretty true across the board, and frankly, you probably didn't get where you are by putting your own needs ahead of your business or your loved ones. What was a strength in your career can manifest as a major weakness in your transition. You have sacrificed the other parts of your life for so many years that planning a meaningful third act gets pushed aside as a soft topic. You need to apply the same skills that made you a successful owner toward planning your next 30 years. Value Acceleration only works if your personal needs receive *equal* attention to your business and financial needs.

If there is one thing I have learned in working with business owners (and as an owner myself), it's that the thought of separating personal from business is ludicrous. Business is personal. It is part of our very nature and a huge part of our identity. Personal goals and objectives, including your family, partners, and the needs of other stakeholders, should be driving the business, not the other way around.

According to Michael Gerber, the noted small business management guru and author of *E-Myth*, finding your personal purpose is what motivates you to get up every morning and slug away. In fact, if you are familiar with Gerber's book, you will note that his business development process starts with a personal question: "What personal purpose is the business serving for you?"

Getting in touch with your personal purpose is vital to having a successful, growing business, and even more so, to building a successful and fulfilling life after you exit. But it requires that you wrestle with things like age and health, personal identity, personal goals, purpose, family responsibilities, lifestyle, community involvement, motivation, and enthusiasm.

Face it, succession is a deeply personal experience. It is complex and emotional. It forces you to deal with your business and personal mortality. It can rob you of your identity. It threatens your sense of purpose and self-worth.

I received a call from Tom, an attorney I work with. He wanted me to meet one of his clients, who he said was "ready" to exit.

"What makes you think he's ready?" I asked.

"He and the wife are burnt out. They've had enough. They are ready to retire and move on," Tom replied easily.

Upon hearing these kinds of statements, I always have a private chuckle.

"Okay," I said, "let's meet with them and see if they are really ready."

The next week I sat down with Tom and his two clients, Ed and Joan, the burnt-out husband and wife. I was initially pleased, thinking it was a good sign that both the husband, the true and sole owner, and his wife were present for the meeting. *Off to a good start,* I thought. After some introductions, discussion about the business, and a little getting to know each other, the conversation evolved.

Chris: "So Tom tells me you are ready to sell."

Ed: "Oh yeah, I'm done. I recently turned 65 and I just can't do it anymore. Time to move on."

Chris: "What do you plan to do after you sell the business?"

Ed: "We're moving to Colorado." Joan was beaming. She looked very happy.

Chris: "Oh, great! Why Colorado?"

Joan: "We love it there. We have been vacationing there for years. We just love the mountains."

Chris: "Cool. Sounds nice. But what are you going to do there?"

Ed: "We're going to build a home and retire there."

Chris: "Excellent! But what are you going to do there?"

Ed: "I just told you. We're going to build a house and retire there."

Chris: "Right, got it. But what are you going to *do* there?"

Ed started to show a little aggravation.

Ed: "I already told you what we're going to do. We're going to retire. What are you getting at?" Joan was not smiling anymore.

Chris: "Well, how long have you owned this business?"

Ed: "For about 35 years."

Chris: "And how many hours a week do you spend working in the business?"

Ed: "It varies, but probably 50, 60, maybe even 70 hours a week sometimes."

Chris: "So let me get this right. You have been working in this business for 50 to 70 hours a week for 35 years and your only plan after you leave this business is that you are going to build a house in Colorado and live there for the rest of your life? How long do you think it will be before you drive each other crazy or die from boredom? Do you know what kind of income you will need to get you through your retirement?"

Ed: "Well, yes, we have some money saved up and once you sell the business, we should have plenty of money, right?"

Chris: "What makes you think the business is salable?"

Ed: "Well, I just assumed someone would want it. After all, it's been producing a nice living for my family for 35 years."

Bad assumption. And on top of that, no personal plan. No written plan. No preparation. What do you think are the chances of succeeding with this transition? And by "succeeding," I don't mean just having enough financial resources to live comfortably even if the business could be sold. Your success in your third act is dependent on being personally fulfilled, having a purpose, and being active after you leave the business.

In contrast, I have lots of really great stories of owners who have exited their businesses and are now living completely different lives and embracing new endeavors. Some of them have dedicated their lives to philanthropy, giving back to the community that helped them succeed. Some of them have started new businesses and even families.

One of my good friends grew a successful tech business and sold it at a premium. He was single all those years, as he dedicated his life to building his business. In his next act, he found love and now he is married and raising two children. His focus has shifted from work to family. And though he has since purchased a new business that he is very passionate about, his new entrepreneurial existence has made more space for things that matter to him personally.

Another owner-friend of mine is in the process of transitioning his businesses to his children. In fact, he shared his experience at an EPI Owners Forum just last year. He explained that he had sort of gone on autopilot, and in turn, so had the business. He has a few health issues and his enthusiasm for the business was diminishing rapidly. He thought that bringing in his children would allow him the opportunity to slow down. Just the opposite happened. The energy and passion exhibited by his much younger children invigorated him. Not having to spend as much time working in the family business allowed him the time and freedom to pursue some other passions that he never had enough time for before. For example, he loves fishing and so he invested in a company that supplies fishing gear. He's also spending more time on his real estate investments, another passion of his.

Owners don't think about these things as much as we should and we tend to neglect these personal matters as our business consumes us. However, it's these personal things that ultimately determine your welfare and happiness. For the most part, the reason that 75% of owners profoundly regretted the decision to exit when responding to the Price Waterhouse survey involved personal reasons, not financial reasons. Most of you don't know what you are going to do after you exit. If you have not planned how to stay relevant, it's highly likely you won't have anything fulfilling in your life anymore…at least from your point of view. You will get bored. And if your next act goes another 30 years, you could be bored for a very long time.

Owners are not the kind of people who sit around much. We are doers. We are busy. We need to be engaged in something. You don't have to be busy with your business in your third act if you don't want to be. Some, myself included, love the game of business. Given a choice, I may never get out of business at all. But, God forbid, if something does happen, I'm going to be ready. And if all goes well, I still have a lot I want to get done. I don't want the grind, or perhaps am not willing to take the risks I used to take. But I definitely want to stay busy, and I definitely want to live a fulfilling life. I'm not done yet.

Owning a business fills up your life. Your identity is tied to it. It is a great source of pride and joy. It keeps you busy and fulfilled. It provides you with a great living. It doesn't cheat on you. It doesn't betray you. It's loyal and steadfast. It's the one place you can go where, in many ways, you think you are totally in control. You have status and respect. The business is a vehicle for expression of your vision and aspirations.

But staying busy in your business also gives you an excuse to ignore the personal things that are gnawing at the back of your brain and poking you in the heart. You're too busy to deal with that soft stuff. You'll deal with it at another time. You think there will be plenty of time to deal with it down the road. Right now, you have a problem in the business that you need to solve... sound familiar?

You can't continue to do this as you approach the needs of your third act. You need to integrate the personal side into the daily operations of your life. You need to spend *equal time* getting in touch with your personal purpose.

BRING PERSONAL PLANNING INTO THE PRESENT

To bring exit planning into the present, begin planning your next act now. By getting started early, you give yourself time to plan your best act properly. I was working with the owners of a business, who, before going into business together, had a serious musical career. At the pinnacle of their previous life, they were nominated for a Grammy Award! What do you think was their passion outside the business? Naturally, it was music. We began to explore this in their personal workshop.

> Chris: "What did you have in mind for what you want to do after you exit?"
>
> Owner #1: "I would like to start a musical institute where we could help children get into music and provide them with coaching so things don't happen to them like they happened to us."
>
> Chris: "Go on, describe it to me."
>
> Owner #2: "We would have a building where we could teach music and voice, provide coaching about the music business, and have a recording studio so we could start recording again."
>
> Chris: "Do you have a written plan for this?"
>
> Owner #1: "Well, no. It's all up in my head. But I can visualize it right now."
>
> Chris: "Okay, one of your personal actions over the next 90 days is to outline, or even better, write a business plan for this musical institute. Let's make it real by putting it on paper. Write a vision and mission statement. Where will the building be located? What's your budget? Where will the funds come from to construct the building and stock it with all the equipment you will need? How will it be staffed? How will you market it?"

These owners had no intention at that time of exiting their business. They knew, of course, they would someday, but not right now.

Chris: "How are you going to fit this in given your current workload with the business?"

Owner #3: "I don't know, but it sure would be nice."

Well, they got very excited about this. Within a few years, they had a building and recording studio, and they were recording a new album. They created time for this because it was their real passion. When I was visiting them several years later, I suggested we meet at ten o' clock the next morning.

Owner #1: "Oh no, I can't do ten. That's my recording time!"

When the time does come for them to exit their business, it will go much smoother and the likelihood that their third act will be their best act is very high.

S.T.E.P.

To get in touch with your personal side, I suggest you play around with a simple exercise called S.T.E.P. It stands for Spiritual, Things, Experiences, and People.

SPIRITUAL

Ask yourself, "What is the source of my inspiration?" Stephen Covey, the author of *The Seven Habits of Highly Effective People,* refers to this as finding your center. He writes, "Whatever is at the center of our life will be the source of our security, guidance, wisdom, and power." He explains that all of us have a center, although many of us may not recognize it or be in touch with it. Some of us may be spouse-centered, family-centered, money-centered, work-centered, possession-centered, friend- or enemy-centered, church-centered, or self-centered. Finding your center is critical to learning about what motivates and inspires you—where your passion comes from.

THINGS

All of us are possession-centered to some degree. We work hard to accumulate "things" that we want. Some of us want wealth, security, cars, homes, private schools, etc. Ask yourself, "What things do I want that I don't have today and what things could I live without?"

EXPERIENCES

To really live life well is to experience life. Ask yourself, "What experiences in my life do I cherish the most? What do I still want to experience someday?" Perhaps it is something on your bucket list. Getting in touch with the experiences you most treasure and those you wish for can be helpful in discovering what is most important to you personally. For me, for example, I think of the birth of my children (family), my marriage to my wife (spouse), attending the Final Four and riding in an Indy car (pleasure), the sale of Flexalloy (money), and the launch of my family business (work). These are some of the experiences that I cherish.

PEOPLE

Finally, think about the people in your life in the past, present, and future. Are there people who have mentored you and helped you, and people you have helped or may want to help? Are there people you wish you could spend more time with? Are there people you need to thank?

One of my clients decided they wanted to sell their business so that they could spend more time with their grandchildren. To them, their grandchildren had become the center of their life. That personal shift motivated them to prepare and then sell their business.

Perhaps one of your personal goals over the next 90 days might be to investigate the abundant literature on this subject. Covey would be a good place to start. Go through the S.T.E.P. exercise over a weekend and try to reconnect with what's really driving you personally. Find out what's important to you. What's your center?

Your Primary Aim, as Gerber has named it, or your personal purpose, "is the vision necessary to bring your business to life and your life to your business. It provides you with a purpose. It provides you with energy. It provides you with the grist for your day-to-day mill."

INTEGRATING THE THREE LEGS INTO A MASTER PLAN

Aligning personal, financial, and business objectives is a core principle on which the CEPA program is built. To succeed today and in the future, you need to make sure that you are giving equal attention to all three legs of the stool. The walk needs to begin by making sure you are in touch with your center and your personal purpose. This personal purpose will identify what your personal financial needs are today and in the future. You will use your business to drive the income and, more importantly, the transferable value to create the financial resources to enable you to achieve your personal purpose and help others.

As Wallace Wattles wrote, "Behind this purpose must be an invincible and unwavering faith that the thing is already yours; that it is 'at hand' and you have only to take possession of it. He who acquires this power becomes a Master Mind. He can conquer fate; he can have what he wants."

In this way, you walk your path to destiny.

CHAPTER SIX

Value ~~Versus~~ AND Income

Business value is the primary long-term goal, not business income. This sounds like a subtle play on words, but in reality, it is a major paradigm shift. Most owners of lower to middle market businesses have "lifestyle" businesses. Lifestyle businesses usually generate a nice income for the owner. But focusing on income alone doesn't mean the business has transferable market value.

This shift in thinking needs to permeate your entire organization. Teaching your employees about the importance of value versus income will bring a different perspective to the business decisions they make every day. The next time one of your managers asks to hire someone, invest in new technology, or buy new equipment, ask them, "What value does this add to the company?" You're likely to receive a blank stare. They won't know what you are talking about because most of

---

Work For Me
Liv Warfield

I started to think how to take some time
To live life and still have peace of mind
When you strive for somethin'
You can make it happen, yeah
That's the way of life
That's the way it is

So I am gonna keep my head in the sky
Put one foot in front of the other
And guide my life
In this life there's struggle
You gotta keep pushin', yeah
It worked for me
It can work for you too

---

them are thinking in terms of fulfilling orders, making product, or paying bills. They don't understand the concept of value creation. And why would they? Have you ever introduced the idea of value creation to them?

> Not long ago, I held a meeting with Chad, a key sales manager for one of my clients. Chad proudly laid out his sales strategy to me. He noted that he had the chance to land a massive new customer that would add a significant amount of revenue for the company. Chad was well-informed; he knew his gross margin and he was fired up.
>
> "What value does landing that customer create?" I asked.
>
> "Uh, are you kidding me? It will add about $4 million in sales and about $2 million in gross margin."
>
> "That's fantastic, congratulations," I said. "But what value does that customer create in terms of its impact on the value of the business?"
>
> He looked at me, confused.
>
> "Okay," I said, "let's take a look. You know this customer will add about $2 million in gross margin or about 50% of sales, yes?"
>
> "Yes."
>
> "What do you think the SG&A expenses will be to land and manage this customer?"

After working through the numbers, we came up with a number of about $1 million: about 25% of sales.

"So the net EBITDA for this client will be around $1 million dollars, right?" I said.

"Yes," Chad responded, highly engaged in this new look at client acquisition.

"Okay, great. And what multiple of EBITDA are we using to value the business?"

"I don't remember," Chad admitted, "But I know you did a business valuation when we started this process last year."

"No problem. We came up with five times EBITDA," I responded, "So what is the value of this customer?"

"$5 million?" Chad answered excitedly.

"Yes, $5 million!" I said, "The generation of $1 million EBITDA is wonderful, but the real value of the customer to the business is $5 million, assuming we set the relationship up so that it is transferable at some point in the future. Sounds like you should pursue it."

"You better believe I will," said Chad.

This concept of value applies across the board. Every time someone says they want to hire someone, you can easily figure out what it will cost in terms of salaries, benefits, and SG&A expenses. If you only concentrate on the expense, you may think twice about hiring that person, because on the surface, it looks like a pure expense. But if you go a step further by asking your team to think about the value being created, it forces them (and you) to think deeper. Consider these questions:

- How will this person impact sales, gross margin, or efficiency?
- What incremental income will be produced by adding this person?
- What is the difference between the cost and the benefit?

This difference between the cost and benefit, multiplied by your EBITDA multiple, is the incremental value. When you look at everyday decisions this way, you might be more apt to make the investment. You may be more willing to ride out the incremental expense for a while until the returns come in—assuming you know how to execute.

Looking back at "The Perfect Exit," when Flexalloy invested 2% of revenue in technology, we certainly didn't expect the investments to pay off right away. That was a lot of money to invest in technology. However, two years later when Andy went to sell the company, the technology was a huge part of why our corporate buyer paid a premium. It just so happened that the corporate buyer was using the same technology as Flexalloy. Only there was a big difference between their technology and ours: Our tech actually worked. Theirs was a mess. They looked at Flexalloy's technology and thought, "If we could deploy this technology in all of our divisions the way Flexalloy has, it will create huge synergies." And that's why the value created from the investments far exceeded the cost.

I teach a short workshop, called *Financials for Non-Financial Managers,* to educate managers about the impact of small everyday decisions on cash flow, profits, and value. I do this because building value is a team sport that requires a paradigm shift and culture change. The only way to really change your culture and get everyone thinking the same way is to integrate value thinking into what you do every day. You need to adopt metrics and reinforce this focused thinking in your daily huddles, your weekly management meetings, your monthly accountability meetings, your quarterly reviews, and your annual strategic planning.

Business valuation should be a mainstay of your business planning. Business value is the baseline measurement of success. You should re-value annually (at a minimum). Even better, do it semi-annually or quarterly. As you read on and learn to navigate the stages of value, consider how well you are integrating this shift in thinking into the daily decisions being made by your managers.

THE FIVE STAGES OF VALUE MATURITY

There are five stages to creating a more valuable business: Identify, Protect, Build, Harvest, and Manage. As you progress through each of the stages using Value Acceleration, your value grows. I call this Value Maturity.

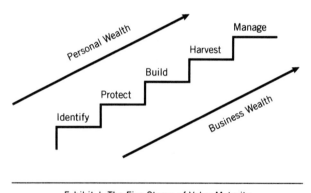

Exhibit J: The Five Stages of Value Maturity

IDENTIFY VALUE

Identifying value is always the first step and should never be skipped. It is completed in Gate One of the Value Acceleration Methodology. Understanding where your business benchmarks in the range of value sets the baseline for everything going forward. This is important for several reasons.

First, as you know, it is likely that 80 to 90% of your net worth is locked up in your business. Second, you need a system which is built to continuously focus your team on maximizing value. Third, the ability to unlock that value at some point in the future will make a significant difference to your lifestyle and, at exit, will fund your next act. Lastly, you need to know this valuation number for business planning, personal planning, and estate and tax planning purposes.

You should have your business professionally valued at least annually. The first time you do this will take a little work and expense. But thereafter, to keep score, you can simply update your most recent year's recasted financial statements; update your personal, financial, and business scorecard; and take another scan of the range of multiples in your industry. But really, you should be doing this continuously anyway. I'll go into this process at length in Section Three. For now, understand that the value of your business and how it benchmarks against others in your industry will identify the value factors that you should focus on to protect what you already have and accelerate the value of your business.

PROTECT VALUE

Once you have identified your baseline value, your next priority is to protect what value you already have by mitigating personal, financial, and business risks. Protecting value is accomplished by creating and implementing prioritized de-risking action plans. In reality, protecting value is the first step in building value. But due to its paramount importance to business owners, I recognize it as a separate stage of Value Maturity.

If you were to do nothing else, mitigating risk alone would improve your business value because valuations are based in part on the real and perceived risks from a buyer's point of view. Actions to reduce risk are common sense and the easiest to implement. You probably love the idea of growing your business, but before you get there, you are more likely concerned about the risks involved, especially if you are over 50.

Review the list below:

Which of these risks do you face from a personal, financial, and business standpoint?

PERSONAL	FINANCIAL	BUSINESS	
Death	Market Risks	Customers	Environmental/Safety
Disability	Diversification	Key People	Technology/Machinery
Divorce	Personal Loans/Debt	Business Interruption	
Health	Personal Lawsuits	Economy	Owner Dependence
Accidents	Loss of Earning Power	Distress	Data/Information
Family Tragedies		Partner Disagreements	Compliance/Legal
	Long-Term Care		Loans/Debt

Exhibit K: Risk Areas

Do you take mitigating your personal, financial, and business risks seriously? Ask yourself the following questions:

- Have I integrated risk management into my management model and personally today?
- Do I take risk seriously enough?
- How much am I willing to risk in order to grow?

Growth is not easy; it's also risky. To grow, you will likely need to put assets at risk (including personal wealth), take on debt, add people, add machinery, and expand facilities. You may need to strategically acquire another company. Understanding your tolerance for risk and willingness to complete actions that protect value is imperative before you begin building value through strategic growth investments. Consider the Five D's: Death, Disability, Divorce, Distress, and Disagreement. Most of us don't think these things will ever happen to us. But do you know that there is a 50% probability that you will be impacted by one of these Five D's? How prepared are you?

Several years ago, the landlord of a building I was leasing walked into the office to see me. We had become friends and I thought he was just stopping by to say hi. I had not seen him for a while and had been wondering where he'd been. He owned several businesses which were doing well and as such, he was well regarded by the business community for his success. He had a net worth of about $12 million and was only 42 years old. He sat down, and I could tell from his demeanor that this visit was not a social one.

> "Chris, you will never believe what happened to me. I made a trip to my home in Florida a few weeks ago (note: this was only his third visit in the last five years because he was so busy all the time). I was really feeling run down and felt like I needed to get away before the busy season hit. As I approached the door, I got a sharp pain in my stomach and then I collapsed. I had to crawl into the house to get to a phone and I called 911. I ended up in the hospital for two weeks with an internal infection. I thought I was going to die. I'm here because I need to change my life. I can't do this anymore. I have to start taking care of myself. I want to start to divest by selling off my businesses, starting with the flagship. I can live off the real estate I own so I'll keep that. But everything else needs to go."

> "Oh my God," I replied. "Are you okay?"

> "No, I'm not. My life is a mess. The businesses are very dependent on me. I work all the time. I've alienated my wife and children. They wouldn't even make the trip with me."

> "Wow," I said. "That's tough. I didn't know things had gotten that bad for you. I'm really sorry to hear that. But I think I can help you."

I explained the process we would need to go through and told him I would draw up the contracts.

After completing a personal, financial, and business assessment and determining where his business placed in the range of value (also known as the Triggering Event), we settled on a target selling price. But I told him I had concerns about his advisory team. His CPA was not cooperative and the process he was using to keep the books updated was ancient. I also noted he did not have a real wealth manager overseeing all his wealth. Everything was disjointed and unorganized. He had no written life-after plan or a financial plan reflecting the income he needed after selling off the businesses. And his attorney was someone he had been using since he started in business 20 years ago. The attorney had officially retired years earlier and was only doing his legal work to make some money on the side.

"The first thing we need to do," I suggested, "is upgrade your advisory team."

So I brought in a new CPA, attorney, and wealth manager who I had been working with through EPI's Northeast Ohio Chapter. The wealth manager, from a prominent local firm, explained that my client's personal financial planning was a mess, but he could get it together. We all got busy preparing him for his next life, starting with selling the flagship.

Over the next several months, my client was in and out of the hospital and his condition was getting worse, both from a health and personal standpoint. His flagship business was seasonal and with all the trips to the hospital, he had virtually missed it. As a result, his sales projections for the coming year were much lower. And because the business was so dependent on him, none of his managers were up to the task of managing the business. Things continued to decline.

I hurried to put a package together to get the business on the market. We agreed to use an auction process to get the business sold as fast as possible. Despite all of our efforts to maintain confidentiality, given the stature of this business in the NEO region, it wasn't hard for the strategic buyers to figure out why we were selling.

"I'm not touching that business," several potential bidders said, "I think I know who it is and he's going down."

The business world can be cruel when they know you are weak.

While this was all going on, my client's wife filed for divorce. This really complicated matters because two years prior, he had put 60% of the business in her name so that the business would qualify for special status when bidding on government work. She didn't have any involvement with the business, but now she and her attorney were quite interested. It was about this time that the real estate market collapsed, leaving his real estate exposed.

Then my friend disappeared. I couldn't reach him. I later learned that he had fallen into a coma and was unresponsive. After a month or so, he came out of it, but was in an extremely weakened state. With everything in his world collapsing around him, he declared bankruptcy and lost most of his $12 million estate. Today he is back; he is alive, but not the same man he was back in the day. His wealth is gone and so is his family and almost everything he once had.

This is a really sad true story. I share it with you because if you have not taken actions to protect your wealth, you could quickly lose it all, just like my friend did. This type of tragedy is never something you expect. But it can happen. It does happen. There is a 50% chance it will happen to you.

BUILD VALUE

I hope that story has compelled you to realize the importance of protecting value. Once you have, you can focus on *building* value.

The difference between protecting and building is that, in the Build Stage, you take a longer-term point of view, prioritizing more strategic actions to increase intangible capital over less strategic actions (a.k.a. de-risking).

Building value results from increases in cash flow (EBITDA) and improvements to your multiple. The multiple is the number assigned by the private capital market to the value of your tangible and intangible assets and the risks associated to your business. As I mentioned, protecting value is also the first step in building value. The second step is improving intangible capital. That is where the opportunity for accelerated value lies and where Value Acceleration can really help you.

Intangible assets are "knowledge capitals" and can be divided into four areas: Human—the value of your talent; Structural—the value of your systems and intellectual property; Customer—the value of your customer relationships; and Social—the value of your brand and culture. Understanding each of the Four Capitals (Four C's) and how you can manage those value factors is critical in your value growth venture. They are broken down for you in Chapter 7.

HARVEST VALUE

At some point in your future, you are going to want to cash in or harvest the value of your business. I have specifically chosen the word "harvest" because it represents the activity of reaping, gathering, and storing something you've grown. As with any growing season, the completion of harvesting marks the end of the growth cycle for a particular crop. In this case, the crop is your business.

Considering your exit options, you may have decided to sell the business to a partner, employees, or family. Or maybe you've decided to sell all or some of it to a private equity firm, family office, or strategic buyer. Your strategy might even be an orderly liquidation, which is a valid option. The key word there is "orderly." A review of the pros and cons of all your options is provided in Section Three. For now, understand that your Value Maturity is determined by how well you understand all of those options. Honestly, you are probably not aware of all your exit options: according to the EPI's *State of Owner Readiness Survey,* two-thirds of all business owners aren't.

It is worth your time to explore the possibilities. Meet a few private equity companies or family offices. Meet with an investment banker. Meet with an ESOP specialist. Learn all you can and take your time.

I have had owners who brought me in to sell their business, and after reviewing all their options, went an entirely different route. I have had owners assume they will transfer the business to a son or daughter only to realize their best option was to sell it, extract the cash, and go in an entirely different direction. This new direction could even mean funding another enterprise that your children are more interested in.

If you haven't already, read *Every Family's Business: Common Sense Questions to Protect Your Wealth* by Dr. Thomas Deans. Tom's position is that selling the business is often your best bet, even if family is involved. And he takes a hard stance on gifting. If you are going to transition to a son or daughter, make them buy it from you at market value.

MANAGE VALUE

The most mature level of Value Acceleration is managing value. Manage Value is the last stage of Value Maturity, but that's not because it comes at the end after you harvest. It's last because it represents full maturity.

You should obviously be managing value through the entire process, not just at the end. If you have identified, protected, built, and harvested value from a personal, financial, and business standpoint, you have managed your value. Managing value begins with identifying it. Remember, to effectively achieve results, it's not just the value of your business you need to manage. You need to manage your personal value and personal financial net worth as well. If you actively manage value through the entire process, you emerge financially independent of your business, with lots of options when the time comes to exit, making the timing of that exit irrelevant. It also preserves those options whether or not the exit is on your terms and timeline.

VALUE MATURITY INDEX

A simple exercise I teach owners at the Roundtables is to create a simple scatter diagram. It can even be handwritten. Keep it simple.

Create a circle and then label five points around that circle.

The labels should be:
- Identify
- Protect
- Build
- Harvest
- Manage

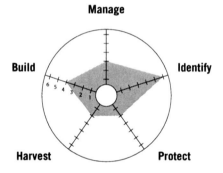

Exhibit L: Value Maturity Index

Now draw a line from the center of the circle to each label. Place six hash marks on each of the lines. Now, number each hash mark, starting from the center and going one through six (six should fall on the most outer layer of the circle).

Now it's time to score yourself! Go through each category and score yourself on how you have been developing your Value Maturity. Be honest. A score of five or six means you would consider yourself best-in-class. A score of one to two means you have done nothing at all or know nothing. A score of three or four rates you slightly above or slightly below average. Note: there is no average.

For example, for the Identify Value Stage, score yourself best-in-class if you:

- You have completed a professional valuation and personal financial and business assessment in the last year.
- You have correlated your assessment and financial analysis to determine where you place in the range of value for your industry.
- You and your core and extended teams deeply understand how a business is valued.
- You have a comprehensive understanding of personal, financial, and business value factors.
- You create prioritized, focused action plans around these value factors every 90 days (focusing on de-risking first), and give them equal attention.
- The 90-day personal and business actions are connected to your personal, financial, and business vision; three-year strategy and one-year initiatives.
- Your management and family are in alignment with your vision and plans.
- You have discussed your valuation with your partner(s), loved ones, and advisory team.

Score yourself a one if you have done nothing at all; award a six if you have fully fulfilled everything you can do in that category. You, like other owners, tend to be overly optimistic, but I'm sure you have a pretty good sense where you actually lie. Once you have gone all the way around the circle, connect the dots between the ranked numbers on each line. This will form another circle inside the outer layer. Now color in this inner circle. What do you see? The space between the outer circle and inner circle is your opportunity for improvement. The larger the shaded area, the higher your Value Maturity. But think positively: the larger the white space, the larger the growth opportunity!

Do this every 90 days. It will take 15 minutes of your time and will remind you of your progress. Each quarter, as you complete actions, your score should increase. That means your shaded area will increase, which means your value is rising. It's pretty straightforward.

To reiterate, there is no "average" and you can't use decimals. If you consider yourself "average," challenge yourself to go further and truly decide if you are slightly above or slightly below. It's hard to be that honest with yourself. It's too easy to say "I'm average." If you have to pick a side of the equator, it makes you think more critically.

Years ago, I learned this scoring system from Peter Hickey of MAUS, an enterprise valuation software entrepreneur, and have found that it initiates thoughtful conversations for owners. More importantly, it is really simple. More details on the value factors that qualify you to be best-in-class are spelled out in the next section.

VALUE ACCELERATION = FOCUS ON THE MULTIPLE

Value acceleration is achieved by focusing on the multiple, which, again, is largely based on the strength of your intangible assets. Calculated value is a fairly simple formula. Here's an easy way to remember:

> **CASH** *(recasted EBITDA)* × **MULTIPLE** *(tangible and intangible assets)* = **VALUE**

Recasted EBITDA (a.k.a. cash) times market multiple equals value (determining recasted EBITDA is pretty easy and I will show you how to do that in Section Three). Obviously, the more cash, the higher the value. Accelerated value, however, is accomplished by raising both the multiple and EBITDA. When EBITDA and your multiple increase simultaneously, you achieve an exponential increase in value.

Every industry trades in a range of multiples. These ranges differ depending on the size of your company, what industry you are in, the state of the private capital market, economic circumstances, and the supply of businesses available in your industry. The range of multiples, for example, in the health care industry is much higher than the range of multiples, say, in energy because of the economic circumstances and the supply of businesses for sale in each of these industries today. A larger company tends to trade at a higher multiple than a smaller company.

The private capital market determines the range of multiples for an industry. You cannot control this. The market controls this range. Weak companies trade at the lower end of the range and others, the premium businesses, trade at the higher end of the range. Your placement, or your specific company multiple in that range, is determined by the perceived strength of your intellectual capital and perceived risks associated to your business. Although you can't control the range, you can control where you place in the range.

YOU CAN HAVE BOTH INCOME AND VALUE

Most owners focus on sales and income only. This is understandable, but misguided. You have realities at play and you are probably asking yourself, "If I can make more income, why wouldn't I do it?"

Focusing on sales and income is important. I am not suggesting it isn't. However, focusing *exclusively* on income is a mistake. Focusing on the multiple is where real value creation lies. Your multiple not only accelerates value, but it also drives income. Focusing solely on income does not necessarily drive value.

> If your business is completely dependent on you to be successful, how much value is there really? Not long ago, I evaluated a $44 million company. The owner turned white when I commented that his business might not have any value.
>
> "How can that be?" he asked.
>
> "Well," I said, "the business relies almost exclusively on you: your relationships with the customer and your ability to drive sales. You have not documented what you do that makes you such a great salesperson and you have no replacement. Past that, you admitted to me that there is only one other person who can drive sales and that the rest of your team was below average at best. You have no contracts with your customers or your suppliers. You have no documentation of your company procedures. You have no awards or community recognition of your accomplishments. You have no brand. The majority of your revenue comes from one customer. You really don't do any marketing. There are few barriers to entry and you don't hold a dominant position in the industry. You have no trademarks or intellectual property."
>
> Stunned silence followed.
>
> "So let me ask you, what exactly would a buyer be purchasing?"

Much of what has been written about exit planning focuses on the endgame. I can't emphasize enough that exit planning is not accomplished by focusing on the endgame. Successful exits are based on what you do every day. There is no reason you can't benefit today *and* in the future. You can do both. You don't have to trade away income for value.

CHAPTER SEVEN

The Four C's

> "...the sum of everything everybody in a company knows that gives it a competitive edge." —Thomas A. Stewart

What is intellectual capital? In his book, *The Wealth of Knowledge,* Thomas A. Stewart defined intellectual capital as knowledge assets: "Simply put, knowledge assets are talent, skills, know-how, know-what, and relationships—and machines and networks that embody them—that can be used to create wealth." It is because of knowledge that power has shifted downstream. This is different from the past, when the power existed with the manufacturers, then with distributors and retailers; now, it resides inside well-informed, well-educated consumers.

It's Yours
Jon Cutler feat. E-man

Acquiring entrance to the temple
is hard but fair
Trust in God-forsaken elements
Because the reward
is well worth the journey
Stay steadfast in your pursuit of the light
The light is knowledge
Stay true to your quest
Recharge your spirit
Purify your mind
Touch your soul
Give you the eternal joy and happiness
You truly deserve
You now have the knowledge
It's Yours

Exhibit M: *Forbes* Top 10 Most Valued Business on the Market in 2016

Rank	Brand	Value	Industry
1.	Apple	$145.3 Billion	Technology
2.	Microsoft	$69.3 Billion	Technology
3.	Google	$65.6 Billion	Technology
4.	Coca-Cola	$56 Billion	Beverage
5.	IBM	$49.8 Billion	Technology
6.	McDonald's	$39.5 Billion	Restaurant
7.	Samsung	$37.9 Billion	Technology
8.	Toyota	$37.8 Billion	Automotive
9.	General Electric	$37.5 Billion	Diversified
10.	Facebook	$36.5 Billion	Technology

If you look at the top 10 most valued companies today, what do they all have in common? They come from different industries, but they all have a commonality. They all have significant knowledge capital which is reflected in their brand value. You could buy a burger anywhere, but McDonald's has a structural process and skilled system for mass-producing their product and service that can be scaled. Coca-Cola has the secret formula that people can't live without; there's a loyalty there. Speaking of brand loyalty, Google, Microsoft, Apple, and even Facebook are companies that people interact with constantly, all day, every day. These are public companies, yes, but the concept of knowledge capital is the same across businesses of all sizes. What makes a brand valuable comes down to the strength of the Four C's.

In the past, wealth was created from physical assets: land, natural resources, and human and machine labor. But technology has disrupted that entire system. Today, wealth is created by your ability to create, transfer, assemble, integrate, protect, and exploit knowledge assets. These are intangible assets.

Stewart further noted, "Because knowledge has become the single most important factor of production, managing intellectual assets has become the single most important task of business."

Looking at the value of a business, you will find that its intangible assets account for most of its value, not its tangible assets. Yet most owners do not get regular feedback on the value of their intangible assets. That is because most accounting systems were built to give you feedback on tangibles. Tax systems were set up for the manufacturing economy of the 1950s, not the high-tech knowledge economy you exist in today.

The value of knowledge assets can be multiplied many times because they can be bought and shared. As management consultant Sid Caesar said, "The guy who invented the first wheel was an idiot. The guy who invented the other three, he was a genius." The essence of value in this new form is its ability to identify, protect, build, harvest, and manage the value of your intangible assets, broken into categories of intellectual capital. Value Acceleration gives you feedback on your management of those assets.

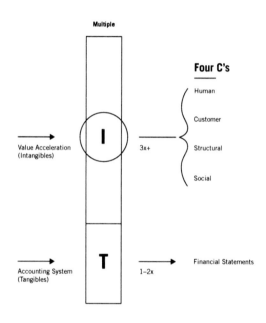

Intangible assets are the sum of your company's intellectual capital, which is divided into four categories: (1) Human, (2) Customer, (3) Structural, and (4) Social. I call them the Four Capitals, or the Four C's.

HUMAN CAPITAL

Human Capital is a measure of the talent of your team. If you have strong talent, someone will place a high value on that. Moreover, if you have really strong, developed talent, your business likely does not depend on you to be successful.

Developing human capital should be your number one priority. It is also likely your biggest headache. In fact, 62% of the owners who attend my Roundtables indicated finding and retaining top talent is the biggest business challenge they face.

Jim Collins, author of classic business books like *Good to Great* and *Built to Last,* emphasized the importance of the power of human capital. Collins coined that lasting and memorable metaphor by comparing a business to a bus and the leader as a bus driver. He rightly states that it is crucial that you continuously consider "First Who, Then What."

He has a linear process for implementing that concept:
1. Get the right people on the bus
2. Get the right people in the right seats
3. Get the wrong people off the bus
4. Put who before what—no matter how dire the circumstances

If you get the right people before you start down the path, your human capital will actually improve your direction, by figuring out who sits where on the bus, and where the bus should be heading.

Jack Welch, the famous leader of GE and arguably one of our country's greatest business leaders in the last 30 years, wrote in his book, *Jack: Straight from the Gut,* "Getting the right people in the right jobs is a lot more important than developing a strategy." He looked for leaders who had the courage to "...kick ass and break glass. We learned the hard way that we could have the greatest strategies in the world. Without the right leaders developing and owning them, we'd get good-looking presentations and so-so results."

DEVELOPMENT CONSIDERATIONS FOR HUMAN CAPITAL

RECRUIT

First, are you recruiting top talent? Why would top talent want to join your company? What makes your company an attractive place to work? Can you clearly articulate this to recruits? What competencies do you need (and already have) to achieve your targets? What core values and personal characteristics are you looking for to ensure new recruits will fit into and contribute to your culture? What does your bench strength (talent pipeline) look like? How are you filling the talent pipeline?

MOTIVATE

Next, what specific things are you doing to motivate your talent? Top talent wants more than "a job." They want to be part of something bigger than that—a cause. They are looking for real passion and a leader who will provide inspiration. Do your core values represent this? Is your core purpose inspirational enough? Can you describe actual experiences and share stories which demonstrate your commitment to these core values and core purpose?

Do you have the right rewards and incentives in place to motivate top talent and keep them motivated? Do you have the right kind of feedback systems to reward top performers and weed out the poor performers? Keeping poor performers around is really demotivating to your top performers. Not financially distinguishing and providing visible recognition to top performers, separating them from those poor performers, is also demotivating.

Wallace Wattles wrote, "Give every man more in use value than you take from him in cash value; then you are adding to the life of the world by every business transaction." If you don't have a financial incentive program in place, you should consider implementing one. If you do have an incentive program, perhaps you should take fresh look at it. Does it reward people for increases in value or just income? Do your people feel entitled to a bonus every year? Or rather, do they understand that good incentive programs are based on the theory of abundance, meaning they are paid only when more resources are created than are consumed?

Top performers not only want and need to be recognized for their contributions to the company, but they deserve to be rewarded financially. The right incentives incite actions that produce results. In this way, incentive programs become self-funded and are earned by successfully completing actions that result in increases in profits and business value. Top talent does not look for handouts. They do not exhibit entitlement behavior. They are willing to earn their way to higher income and possible equity by being vested in the success of the company. A great book on this subject is *Ownership Thinking* by Brad Hams.

However, financial incentives are not enough. What are you doing outside the business to build teamwork and culture? Are your teams getting enough education and training? Have you made it clear how to advance within the company? Top talent wants to be in an environment where they can continuously learn and grow. Have you created this kind of environment?

RETAIN

How well do you retain top talent? What are the turnover rates of high performers and poor performers?

At Price Waterhouse, we had a performance rating system that scored performance on a scale of one to five. One was the highest, five was the lowest, and three was average. And at PwC, being average meant you were not going to be there long. I recall receiving a "3" on my first assignment about four months into the job. As an experienced hire from the corporate world, I was used to an aggressive, thou-shalt-do-this, management approach. Part of my management style was driven by the environment at Sherwin Williams, where I felt like I was one of the smartest people in the room most of the time.

One of the best things about working for PwC was being surrounded by a surplus of really smart people, most of whom seemed a lot smarter than me. I loved it because, for the first time, I felt like I was learning rather than teaching. However, one of the biggest lessons I learned was that if you want to get the best performance and retain top talent, you can't manage highly intelligent talent the same way you manage average employees. You need to inspire them, challenge them, give them honest feedback, help them grow, and provide incentives to reward their performance.

On my next assignment, working for Phil Andrews, I was rated a "2." And by the time I received my third review, Phil scored me a "1." From thereafter, I was a "1 performer." And the PwC policy was that you never lost a 1 performer... *ever*. When I announced to the partners that I had decided to leave, they threw everything they could at me to keep me. And I tell you this to emphasize that you need to have specific strategies, goals, and metrics which measure retention and attrition—not only of your top talent, but also of the worst.

In addition to providing a path for professional growth, you should consider providing retention incentives to key employees. Retention incentives are tied to value growth, not just income. They provide the opportunity for your superstars to benefit from value creation. There are a variety of forms of retention programs, too diverse to go into in this book. However, it would be worth your time to investigate them. Typically, they do not require capital investment by the employee. They are designed to reward employees based on value creation and are realized upon some form of triggering event, like the sale of your business. Notably, they typically have a vesting process which incentivizes key people to stay with the company.

EVOLVE

The final thing you must consider is how your team needs to evolve. I imagine you would prefer to promote from within if you can. And most of the time, you can if you have the right management development processes in place. Occasionally, you may need to reach outside to acquire knowledge that is not present in your business when you can't wait for it to be developed. That's what Andy Rayburn at Flex did when staging "The Perfect Exit." He reached outside his organization to hire me, with my IT and supply chain experience, and our CFO, who brought prior sell-side experience.

Verne Harnish stated that when a business doubles in size, its complexity increases by a factor of 12. Whether promoting from within or bringing in outside talent, your leadership team needs to be able to evolve as your business evolves. And all their people need to evolve as the leadership team evolves, and so on down the line.

VITALITY CURVE

I love the way Jack Welch measured talent at General Electric (a company that still sits in the top 10 most valuable companies today). I have adopted a version of his methodology since I first read his book, *Jack: Straight From The Gut*. Welch described GE as a people factory. He was extremely proud of the talent at GE, and he knew developing it was his number one job.

> "We build great people, who then build great products and services." —*Jack Welch, General Electric*

In looking for a better way to evaluate the organization, he came up with the term "differentiation" to sort out the A, B, and C players. These A, B, and C players were ranked on a "Vitality Curve."

"A" players are people who are filled with passion, committed to making things happen, and open to ideas. They have the ability to energize themselves and everyone who comes in contact with them. They make business productive and, at the same time, fun. At GE, "A" players had "the four E's": high *energy* levels, the ability to *energize* others, the *edge* to make tough yes-or-no decisions, and the ability to *execute*. These four E's were directly connected by one P... *passion*.

It was passion, more than anything else, that separated "A" players from "B" players. "B" players are the heart of the company and are key to operational success. The "C" player was the person who can't get the job done, described as someone who would "enervate rather than energize."

GE would classify people into the Top 20, the Vital 70, and the Bottom 10. Most of your time and attention should be spent on the Top 20 and Bottom 10. Don't worry too much about the Vital 70; they will go along with whatever. They show up, do their job, and go home. They are vital because they are needed. But they will not elevate your culture or your business to the next level, and in turn, they will never be able to replace you. Although you want to give everyone an opportunity to learn and grow into a leader, most of your Vital 70 are not interested.

It's the Top 20 who really carry the company. They are the ones with passion. They don't need to be motivated; they *are* motivated. They self-motivate and spread motivation. Remember "First Who, Then What"? They are the "Who." They drive the bus. They determine the direction of the bus. They determine who sits in what seats. The Top 20 should be getting raises, bonuses, and recognition far exceeding that of the Vital 70.

At GE, just like at PwC, losing a Top 20 player was a sin. At GE, the turnover rate for "A" players was less than 1%. The Bottom 10 are the players that need to be turned over. You should look to replace a Bottom 10 with a potential Top 20 every time. Over time, by regularly following this routine, you will continuously improve the strength of your human capital because the bar is always being raised. Price Waterhouse used a similar model. I have deployed this model within my own businesses, and with several clients, and it proves to be true almost every time.

Welch and GE have received some criticism that this Vitality Curve model is cruel and cold. But Welch felt very differently: "What I think is brutal and 'false kindness' is keeping people around who aren't going to grow and prosper. The characterization of vitality curve as cruel stems from false logic and is an outgrowth of a culture that practices false kindness. Performance management has been a part of everyone's life from the first grade. Differentiation applies to football teams, cheerleading squads, and honor societies. It applies to the college admission process...it applies at graduation when honors like summa cum laude or cum laude are added to your diploma. There is differentiation for all of us in our first 20 years. Why should it stop in the workplace, where most of our waking hours are spent?"

I strongly agree with Jack. There is absolutely room for kindness in valuable businesses, but false kindness? No.

Some might argue that programs like GE's only apply to big corporations, but again, I disagree. These principles can be applied to any size of organization. I am a lower middle market business owner and it absolutely applies to my company. And I'll bet if you look at your organization right now, about 20% of your people are carrying the organization and creating its culture, about 10% of them are marginal performers at best, and about 70% will go along with whatever you ask them to do. I see it over and over. Size doesn't matter. You can have 20 people or 2,000 people and it almost always comes pretty close to this split. So as an owner focused on increasing the value of your business, focus your attention on your "A" and "C" players and you will build your human capital.

CUSTOMER CAPITAL

> "The basic goal of any strategy is simple enough: to win the customer's preference and create a sustainable competitive advantage, while leaving sufficient money on the table for shareholders."
> —Larry Bossidy and Ram Charan, the authors of Execution

Consider these questions in looking at the value of your customer capital:
- How strong are your relationships with customers?
- Are you integral to your customers' success because the products and/or services that you offer are unique?
- Are these relationships deep, long-term, and contractual?
- Are the relationships delivered in a consistent, reliable, recurring fashion?
- Most of all, are these relationships transferable?

If you can answer yes to those questions, you have strong **customer capital.** Recurring revenue, in particular, is highly regarded. In *E-Myth,* Michael Gerber writes, "...the Entrepreneurial Model does not start with a picture of the business to be created, but of the customer for whom the business is to be created."

Ask yourself: How does your business look to the customer today? How does it stand out? What three things would a customer say you do well? What three things would a customer say you should start doing? What three things would a customer say you should stop doing?

Everything starts with the customer and getting a clear picture of that customer. In fact, how the business interacts with customers is more important than what it sells.

Be aware of the risk of "customer concentration." If one customer accounts for more than 25% of your total revenue, it actually reduces your value—sometimes to the point that it is a deal killer. Your relationships can be strong and they might never think to leave your customer book, but frankly, the risks trump the relationship. This is a common occurrence in middle market companies: to have customer concentration issues without much option for diversification. So what do you do? You can make your relationships so entangled that your customers can't live without you. Plus, add sales contracts (building transferability) and you reduce your concentration risks.

STRUCTURAL CAPITAL

Structural capital is the business's infrastructure. It comprises the systems and tools that augment the customer and human capital on which your company is built. It has two purposes. First, it takes what exists inside your brain and turns it into a transferable form. These are the best practices that can be purchased and repurposed.

The second purpose of structural capital is to "...connect people to data, experts, and expertise—including bodies of knowledge—on a just-in-time basis (Thomas A. Stewart)." Structural capital captures the knowledge assets within your company, converting that mental process into company property and, therefore, makes it transferable. Knowledge assets include the people, processes, and technology, as well as intellectual property, that enable your team to do the things that make them so special, allowing them to meet and exceed customer expectations, and enabling them to build and sustain these lasting and recurring relationships.

Your knowledge needs to be documented and transferable, such that someone else can learn from you and apply it. Making this knowledge company property ensures that when your talent walks out the door at night, the knowledge they house doesn't walk out the door with them.

I like to divide structural capital into four areas: processes, people, technology, and facilities. Ask yourself: Are there specific processes, people, technology, and facilities that we deploy that make us special? Are these well documented to the point that they are transferable and someone will want to pay a premium to get them?

SOCIAL CAPITAL

Finally, and arguably most importantly in today's world, there is **social capital.**

Bossidy and Charan, authors of *Execution: The Discipline of Getting Things Done,* considered social capital the "Social Operating System." It represents your culture, your brand, the way your team works, the rhythm of the day-to-day operations and communications, and the way you communicate with customers. All of us have seen flashes of this in the market. Great companies like GE, Apple, Google, and even Flexalloy all have high social capital. These companies have moxie, a vibe. You feel it as soon as you walk on the property. You know there is something special about them. And it's reflected in their market value. Social capital is hard to measure and it takes years to discover it. But you know it when you have it.

When you have built and packaged your intellectual capital, your business has replaced you, which is a good thing. It's not about you anymore; it's about the business. Your business now becomes the product versus the products or services you sell.

CASE STUDY: FLEXALLOY

THE COMPANY

Flexalloy was in the business of just-in-time distribution of fasteners to trucking and heavy equipment manufacturers... or was it?

When I joined Flexalloy, it was doing around $93 million in sales. Within three years, Flexalloy achieved around $265 million in sales, a compound annual growth rate of 42%. This was all organic growth. Because the company was private, I can't share with you what it sold for. However, a reasonable estimated valuation at $93 million in sales might have been $46 million. At $265 million, a reasonable average valuation would be $132 million: an increase of $86 million in just three years. What I can tell you is that Flexalloy sold at a much higher price than that because it was a premium company and, as such, earned a premium multiple. Let's explore what made Flexalloy so valuable.

Managing fasteners for the manufacturers was a real pain. You have thousands of five- and ten-cent parts. Yet these parts were in the top five bill of materials on every piece of machinery being assembled. The last thing you wanted to do was shut a line down because you ran out of a five-cent part. So what did the manufacturers do? They stockpiled them, of course, carrying excessive amounts of inventory and tying up excessive amounts of financial resources. When an engineering change hit, they were stuck with all these obsolete parts, now forced to write off far too much. Further, if you took all of the physical assets of Flexalloy combined, they accounted for a fraction of what was spent to acquire the company. So the question is, why did our corporate buyer pay so much more than Flex's tangible physical asset value?

The answer: **intellectual capital.**

I am not suggesting you don't have to invest in physical assets. You do. At Flex, we invested in traditional physical assets like facilities, equipment, IT, trucks, and bins. But the investment in physical assets is not enough. The exponential value of Flex was created through the knowledge capital of how optimize the use of these physical assets. We had to figure out how to deploy them in such a fashion that it would eliminate waste (without assuming the burden) and improve the flow of our customers' assembly lines.

We had to reduce the financial capital and improve our customers' ability to produce more product in less time. To accomplish this goal, we had to:

- Reduce the number of suppliers
- Improve supply chain flow
- Improve quality
- Reduce waste
- Engineer better parts
- Improve on-time delivery
- Replace their systems with ours

It was our knowledge of how to do it that made the difference. We figured it out. Our knowledge trumped the manufacturer's knowledge, which allowed us to displace them in the supply chain. What the customers were really buying was our knowledge, not our supply.

THE TALENT

Andy already had great talent at Flex when I joined. But he was missing a few elements he needed to round out his team: (1) a strong IT guy who understood supply chain management and (2) a strong financial guy with the experience and know-how to position a company to sell at a premium. The company didn't depend solely on Andy. Granted, the company thrived on his personality; he was a great leader. But the key was we didn't need Andy to fulfill our mission.

Andy had a very flat organization made up of several directors who reported to him. The directors included finance, IT, operations, engineering, and two sales directors. We would meet with Andy every Monday from ten o'clock to noon. There was rarely an agenda. The purpose of the meeting was to just sit down as a team and talk about what was going on, resolve conflicts, figure how we were going to solve problems, and simply talk to each other. After that, we might not see Andy the rest of the week.

We were empowered to do what we needed to hit one brand promise objective: "99.99% on-time delivery." Obviously hard to do, but it was a pretty simple focus. And the teams that worked for us were handpicked to fit into our culture.

THE CUSTOMERS

We had tremendous customer capital. The key to our solution was to get our customers to single-source *all* fastener components to us. We provided what we called "delivery at the point of use." If you worked on the line at one of the factories we supplied, all you had to do was turn around, grab a fastener from the point of use bin, and install it. Everything before that was handled by Flex.

We had satellite facilities within minutes of our customers. Every two hours, one of our employees would scan the bins and send a signal back to the satellite, which would initiate an order and send a truck over to replenish the bins. We handled the inventory, the quality, the purchasing, and the freight—everything prior to point of use.

Even if a customer wanted to replace us, which they never did, can you imagine how difficult it would be? We were deeply entangled into our customers' businesses. We were so intertwined; you couldn't tell whether the employee in the factory was ours or theirs. We were an integrated part of each customer's team.

We dominated the market, capturing most of the large trucking and heavy equipment manufacturers. The manufacturers hated it because we were able to insert ourselves between them and the customer, lessening their customer capital. We controlled the flow of product. We consolidated suppliers, which drove down costs. We inserted technology to make our processes more efficient, and we trained our people extremely well. Flexalloy was a premier company in many ways, and this was clearly expressed by what our corporate buyer paid for it.

THE SYSTEMS AND PROCESSES

Our intellectual capital went beyond talent and customers. Flex knew that in order to scale at a compound annual growth rate of 42%, we needed to upgrade our systems and processes. Strategically, we sold off the manufacturing component of the business, and focused only on just-in-time distribution. We invested 2% of revenue into information technology, upgrading everyone's ability to perform.

Our slogan was "FlexAbility" to reflect that the system focus was to improve everyone's ability to serve the customer. We documented all our processes, and got ISO 9000 certified. We did all of this in a three-year period. And all of this structural capital was transferable.

THE CULTURE

Socially, you could not find a better place to work. The culture had already been developed when I arrived. We held "In the Paint" company-wide meetings every month. We moved to a brand-new, custom-built, beautiful facility. Our employees were called partners, and were treated as such. Andy had a dugout suite at Jacobs Field. Every Friday, we would have a drawing so that a group of employees would have a chance to attend a ballgame in the suite. Every single employee had an opportunity to enjoy that privilege.

We had a program called CARE: Customers Always Receive Excellence. Each department had a nickname and competed in the quarterly CARE Challenge. I ran IT, and my team was called "The Hard Drivers." To compete in the CARE Challenge, each department was asked to prepare a set of customer-oriented improvement initiatives.

A big board displaying a racetrack was positioned at the facility's entrance so everyone could see it, with each department's nickname on a horse. As you completed your initiatives, your horse would move toward the finish line. Whoever won the quarterly challenge received their pick of any restaurant to take their entire department out to dinner. Andy would provide a limousine to take the group back and forth to the restaurant. Also visible to everyone every day, and posted on the wall near the CARE Challenge board, was our service challenge: 99.99% on-time service.

What I remember most is that, although we had our competitive battles day to day, when the chips were down and we were in trouble, our departments put that all aside and pooled together to solve the problem quickly. I remember one of the corporate buyer executives, a member of their buy-side team, telling me that one of the big things they really valued was the potential to leverage that kind of culture throughout all of their facilities, on top of coveting our customer relationships, our talent, and our structural capital. Flexalloy used knowledge capital to create human, customer, structural, and social capital, driving the value of the company sky-high.

TRANSFERABILITY IS THE KEY

Value can only be harvested if your intellectual capital is transferable. Ask yourself:
- Is your business transferable?
- Is your talent transferable?
- Are your customer relationships transferable?
- Are your processes and technology transferable?
- Can someone else learn them?
- Is your culture so deep that integrating your team into your buyer's business would raise the bar, providing them the opportunity to perform like you do?

The only way you "cash in" on your most valuable asset is to transfer it to someone who will pay you a premium because they have not been able to duplicate what you have done. Or maybe they don't want to spend the years or the money to get to that place. It's a lot easier to scale a business than it is to start a business, especially if you can leverage a successful model. Having a model right in front of you that is already proven and leverageable into operations is extremely valuable to a buyer.

Well, I am not going to sell the business, you say, so I don't need to worry too much about driving up my Four C's. But you will still transfer it. Perhaps to family, a partner, a management team, or to employees. And if you choose any of the inside options, you will not have a big liquidity event at the time of your exit. But you will need the business to perform as well, or even better, when you are not there working in it, in order to get all of your money out of it.

The business may have been producing a very nice income for you over the years. But you will never get four, five, or six times or more than the EBITDA it generates if someone can't continue doing what you have been doing. There must be continuity. The option you choose is irrelevant; the business needs to continue to produce high results without you there. What you have created has to be transferable.

If you personally own all the customer relationships, if the talent at your company will only work for you or cannot produce without your guidance, then there is nothing to transfer. When you go away, the relationships go away and therefore so will the business.

Remember, you are transferring a projected stream of income with the potential for this stream of income to get even better after you are gone. If that income goes away or gets reduced when you extract yourself, then there is limited value, if any value at all.

Having a strong management team, a high degree of customer capital, well-documented systems and processes, and a winning culture doesn't just benefit you at exit. A transferable business benefits you right now. It will drive more sales and income. It makes you independent, which adds personal value. It frees you to take more leisure time to sustain yourself or to spend being creative. You are free to spend more time working on your business instead of in it.

It develops your team so that the business can run without you. Be aware of your exit options, but move toward building transferability. You can create a transferable business by taking action now, and you will benefit from those actions today, as well as in the future.

CHAPTER EIGHT

Relentless Execution

> *"By thought the thing you want is brought to you, by action, you will receive it."* —Wallace Wattles

At the end of the day, knowledge capital is worthless if it is not expressed in action. Larry Bossidy and Ram Charan wrote in the book *Execution*, "Most often today the difference between a company and its competitor is the ability to execute. Execution is the greatest unaddressed issue in the business world today. Its absence is the single biggest obstacle to success..."

Execution is more than a set of tactics. It is a **discipline;** a system that needs to be built into a company's strategy, goals, and culture. Ask yourself: Does my company regularly produce expected results? If not, you need better execution. If you are not producing results regularly, it means one of two things: (a) your team is not capable of making them happen (they don't have the skill, knowledge,

---

Working Man
Rush

I get up at seven, yeah
And I go to work at nine
I got no time for livin'
Yes, I'm workin' all the time

It seems to me
I could live my life
A lot better than I think I am
I guess that's why they call me
They call me the workin' man

---

or willpower); or (b) you have misjudged the challenges they face to make them happen.

In my experience, most of you inherently know what would make your business stronger and what you need to do to accomplish that. Strategies are not often wrong. More often, the issue is that they fail to be executed. You may have failed to consider how to actualize the changes needed, the complexity of the change, the resources required, and the paradigm shifts needed to succeed. Ask yourself: Do I have a systematic approach to deal with setbacks, resistance, and constraints—physical, mental, and emotional—to overcome the hurdles to succeed? Many thought leaders have written about what needs to be accomplished to create a more valuable business. But when you ask them how to do it, the dialogue goes dead. Few spell out how or what they actually mean. According to Bossidy, you need to keep three things in mind:

1. No worthwhile strategy can be planned without taking into account the organization's ability to execute it.
2. Execution is a systematic process of rigorously discussing the hows and whats, questioning, tenaciously following through, and ensuring accountability.
3. You need robust dialogue, accountability, and follow-through.

A CULTURE OF RELENTLESS EXECUTION

In my companies, we live by a core value we call **relentless execution.** When choosing and setting priorities, we get into the details. Who will be responsible? What are our options? What are the deliverables? Where are the resources going to come from? What are the risks? What are the milestones that will demonstrate we are on track? Furthermore, our action plans are scoped within reasonable delivery timelines. Big projects are broken down into incremental, 90-day periods (90-day sprints, we call them) of delivery, accountability, and recalibration. In other words, our system is built to be fast and flexible.

Today's business environment is always throwing curves at you. Granted, you need to set long-term direction with vision, purpose, and targets that you keep at the top of your mind. To stay connected to it, you should revisit that vision every 90 days. Does it still make sense or does it need to change given what you have learned over the last 90 days? As you implement the vision in 90-day cycles of improvement (called Quarterly Renewals), assess your accomplishments and disappointments, then align and recalibrate a new set of priorities for the next 90-day sprint. You need a fast strategy, with a continual loop of setting, executing, measuring, reconnecting, and recalibrating action every 90 days. If you do this, you have developed a culture of relentless execution.

With an execution mindset and strong human capital, you won't even have to tell your people what to do. Instead, you become a conditioning coach for leaders. You ask questions so that your team can figure out what to do on their own. As Bossidy writes in *Execution*,

> *"In this way she coaches them, passing on her experience as a leader and educating them to think in ways they never thought before. Far from stifling people, this kind of leadership helps them expand their own capabilities for leading."*

This is what Jim Collins was referring to when he emphasized "First Who, Then What." If you have secured the right talent, cultivating a culture of relentless execution is your next priority.

Execution needs to be practiced, and staff needs to be held accountable. Your management team and key employees have to be involved in establishing priorities prior to executing them. People need to be educated and your management systems, like Value Acceleration, need to provide them regular feedback. Accountability does not mean that you beat your people up for missing goals. *Accountability is a learning process.* If your team made the goal, ask why. What did we do right? If you missed, why? What did we do wrong? Which assumptions were incorrect? Which resources were promised, but not provided? How can we do better the next time?

Your key role in this process is teacher. Good leaders regard every encounter as an opportunity to teach. With this in mind, consider your methods for acknowledging positive performance. You not only want to measure accomplishment; you want to influence behavior. If your company rewards based on achievement and accomplishing action (demonstrated by deliverables) and promotes people for execution, your culture will change.

Some staff just don't produce—ever. These people are the Bottom 10 and need to be changed out. But in most cases, not delivering on an action is due to choosing the wrong priority or some unanticipated problem, rather than lack of staff commitment. You may have estimated wrong or had another opportunity pop up that you needed to get on right away. These things happen. But when they do, it should not take you completely off course. This is why the Value Acceleration Methodology recalibrates every 90 days. Sometimes you absolutely do have to change your people, but most of the time, lack of execution is a systematic problem.

Execution is based in reality. Many years ago when I worked for The Sherwin Williams Company, I took on a project at the Morrow, Georgia, plant to improve cycle time by 20% with minimal investment in equipment and facilities. We started the process with analysis, selecting a sample of key products, setting standard cycle times for each stage of production, and standard wait times between each of these stages. We made assumptions based on the formulations and the equipment on the floor. Next, we began to measure deviations to the assumed standard. The deviations were facts based in reality. We would sort through the list, focusing on the products that had the greatest deviations. We would meet with the floor crew to get their input to find out why—what happened? Then we would reset the standard, if appropriate, and run another series of deviations. We continued using this Learn-Practice-Test process for months, consistently narrowing down the causes and the number of deviations until we got them into reasonable range. By consistently looking at real data, challenging our assumptions, and being persistent, we were able to produce results and dial in the processing times. Within nine months, we accomplished our objective, improving cycle time with a fraction of the investment that would have been required to expand capacity by adding physical equipment and facilities. That was real value creation.

Execution requires discipline grounded in action. Following sequential steps to getting things done keeps you moving, and moving in the right direction. Taking the time to organize before you execute will help clarify your capabilities and determine what you should be executing first, second, and third, ultimately ensuring you are working on the right things.

THE IMPORTANCE OF PURPOSE

I can't emphasize enough the importance of vision and purpose. Your business is a living, breathing thing. It is driven by people who share your vision, and who create and execute processes and systems to deliver extraordinary services and products to your customers. These customers place a high value on the experience of doing business with you, not just your products and services. The way you do business is a reflection of your culture. This vision, alignment, accountability, and rhythm are the raw materials that make up that culture and the customer experience. If your team is connected to your vision, they will be more passionate, more creative, and more committed. **Vision sustains action.**

If you commit to a creating a culture of accountability, you will get things done. And if you don't get things done, you will be able to analyze why. Your metrics will reflect your priorities so that all of your employees understand your definition of success in clear terms. And finally, if you create routines, fostering better communication, providing guidelines for how things should flow and how people should behave, and you repeat these patterns until they become second nature, your company will be both effective and efficient.

Before goals comes purpose. Purpose expresses personal values, inspires and unifies the team, focuses action, and disciplines you to think strategically. When your company lacks purpose, good people leave. Purpose is energizing and energy attracts people who are willing to subordinate individual agendas to the group's agenda. Guys like Rayburn and Christman have purpose. That's why I have been willing to bust my butt for them. In *Managing the Dream,* Bennis wrote:

> *"All leaders have the capacity to create a compelling vision, one that takes people to a new place, and the ability to translate that vision to reality."*

Purpose is a reflection of your vision. In creating vision, you need to consider personal and financial goals, including your health, family responsibilities, partner and family situations, and community involvement, as well as the business life cycle, the market, and the source of your enthusiasm and passion. Start by asking yourself a simple question: **What does success mean to me?**

Wallace Wattles wrote in *The Science of Getting Rich,* "You must form a clear and definite mental picture of what you want; you cannot transmit an idea unless you have it yourself. Behind your clear vision must be the purpose to realize it; to bring it out intangible expression. And behind this purpose must be an invincible and unwavering faith that the thing is already yours; that it is 'at hand' and you have only to take possession of it. You do not make this impression by repeating strings of words; you make it by holding the vision with unshakable purpose to attain it, and with steadfast faith that you do attain it."

Creating a compelling vision is a must! To test the strength of your vision, start by considering these four words: Belief, Passion, Opportunity, and Focus.

BELIEF

If you don't have a vision, STOP! Go develop one. If you do, challenge your level of belief.

- Do you really believe in it?
- Are you willing to sacrifice and invest in it?
- Are you willing to accept the risks to achieve it?
- Do you really believe it will pay off? Why?

Do some soul searching. Examine your motives. Why do you believe it?

First you have to believe it. Only then will others believe in it. Colin Powell once said, "Optimism is a force multiplier." Your belief in your vision and your ability to communicate it are a compelling force.

PASSION

Passion is compelling. Passion gets you through the difficult times. Passion gives you the resolve to persevere. And it makes what you are doing fun. It's not work if it's fun. Are you passionate about your vision?

OPPORTUNITY

What is the opportunity? Try to be as specific as possible in describing it.
- What will the organization look like in three to five years?
- What kinds of people are working for you?
- What kinds of customers are you selling to? How many? How much? Where?
- What products and services are being offered? Where in the market are you dominating the competition or can you dominate?
- How has your role changed?

Challenge your thinking. Do these things seem realistic? Why? Be as clear as you can be without overthinking it. But have enough specifics for it to feel real and to enable others to see what you see.

FOCUS

If you have been able to define the opportunity with enough detail, you are likely passionate and you really do believe you can do this. You are now ready to focus on how to get it done.

Focus takes the intangible and makes it tangible. Focus is needed to keep you on track. Focus defines the specific roadmap of activities needed to begin the journey. When developing your focused vision, consider these principles of growth:

- Growth is a result, not an action. Don't pursue growth; follow through on actions that will result in growth.
- Understand what you are getting into. Studies haves shown that each time a company doubles in size, the people, process, and technology complexity increases by a factor of 12. Ouch! In my experience, this is a major reason growth plans can't be sustained or companies experience choppy growth.
- Use the Business Planning Pyramid to think through your plan—you must have a plan.
- Are you capable of providing the right kind of leadership and do you have the right people in the right seats on the bus? Read more in the book *Good to Great* by Jim Collins.
- Having the right people is vital to leveraging your time and focusing it on growth. Your people will need to step up, and so will their people, and so forth.
- Invest in your people. Create personal and professional development plans to develop talent and promote as often as you can from within.
- Every manager must create more resources than they consume.
- Memories are short; reward incrementally and often.
- Use the Value Acceleration Methodology to create focus and capture the framework of your vision.
- Is your vision linked to your one-year objectives and quarterly priorities?
- Are your priorities clear? Have you aligned and set accountabilities with the management and personal planning teams? At this point, I'm assuming that you have the right team.
- Is the plan integrated into the daily, weekly, monthly, quarterly, and annual routines of the company and your life?
- What are two to three metrics that will demonstrate your plans are on track?

- Have you established monthly team accountability reports where core team members report progress on their accountable areas?
- Create a visual/storyboard which communicates the vision and progress to everyone in the company.
- Meet with your management and personal planning teams off-site one day each quarter and recalibrate. Are the goals still appropriate? How did we do? What did we learn? What must we start or stop doing? Use a facilitator so you can participate.

Your vision and purpose should be aligned with your core values. To ensure you have a true set of core values, stop right now and ask yourself: Can we specifically tell stories that demonstrate our commitment to our core values? Take a few minutes. Then express this in the statement of a brand promise. You should be able to express your brand promise on one sheet of paper by creating a few sentence statements for each of the following four questions:

Mission: What is our mission?
Reason to Believe: Why do we believe we can achieve it?
Proof: What proof do we have to back up this reason to believe?
Tone and Manner: What is the experience going to be like (behavior)?

Next, ask yourself: In which two areas of the marketplace can my company dominate? Focus on being the best at something.

In the old economy, companies tried to optimize balance between price and services. Most resided somewhere in the middle. But over the last several decades, companies have moved either left (to compete on price) or right (to compete on specialization).

Brand Statement (April 26)

Mission. We provide innovative, process-oriented professional services that help clients get better returns from their technology investments by improving organizational ability and aligning people and technology through business processes, creating tech-savvy organizations that make their businesses faster, more efficient, and more profitable.

Reason to Believe. We are professionally seasoned and experienced in managing complex technology portfolios for growing organizations. We have expertise in supply chain management systems and processes, process engineering, change management, project and program management, and strategy development. Our knowledge base encompasses multiple industries, best practices, and development of organizational learning programs.

Proof Statement. We have successfully delivered multiple package and custom software developments, ERP selections and implementations and participated in the development and implementation of logistics solutions for small and large organizations as senior members of executive management teams within organizations and in third party situations.

Tone and Manner. We provide people who are business solution-oriented, focusing on the customer, people, and processes before technology. We are problem solvers, practical, financially sensitive, persistent, energetic, and enthusiastic about what we do. We are "success junkies," thriving on challenge and the success of our clients.

Exhibit O: Brand Statement

The mass-market strategies of the left-moving companies have resulted in many of our big-box retail outlets of today, companies like Wal-Mart, Sears, and Home Depot. Their primary driver is price reduction. They offer an array of products as cheaply as possible, and capture as much of the consumer's dollar in one place as they can. But if you are not a big-box, like most of you reading this, you are unlikely to be able to compete on price. If you are a middle market business, your strategy should be specialization, where you compete on service and the deployment of knowledge capital. So again, ask yourself, considering that price is not an option, in what two areas can you dominate?

At the time they purchased Flexalloy, our corporate buyer was a $14 billion, multi-national organization. The business unit that purchased us was 20 times our size. The reason they wanted us so badly was for our specialization, which we produced through the application of knowledge. Nobody in the industry could distribute fasteners at the speed and quality that we could.

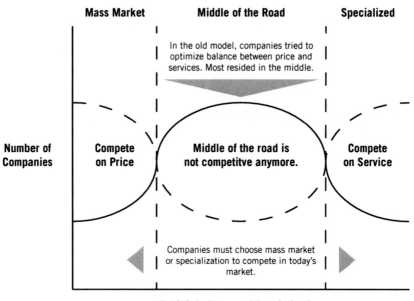

Exhibit P: Degree of Specialization

THE IMPORTANCE OF PLANNING—SETTING GOALS AND OBJECTIVES

Goals, objectives, and targets should be set at three to five years, one year, and 90 days. The three- to five-year goals should be visionary, focusing on the competencies that you need to develop to reach your targets.

Ask yourself: What three to five capabilities or competencies does my company need to develop to reach our targets and achieve our vision? These competencies could be in any number of functional areas, including but not limited to: Customers, Marketing, Sales, Customer Service, Fulfillment, Operations, Human Resources, Information Technology, Facilities, Processes, Finance, and Legal.

I created a model called the **Business Planning Pyramid** to provide guidance on building integrated business plans that drive business value. It can help you figure out the competencies you need to develop over the next three to five years.

This pyramid will help you build integrated business strategies, right down to the specific sales channel if that's where you want to go. I also use this model to divide a company into its functional components and the value factors that drive you to be best-in-class. Furthermore, the model has metrics. You can score yourself in each of the categories on a regular basis to measure value creation.

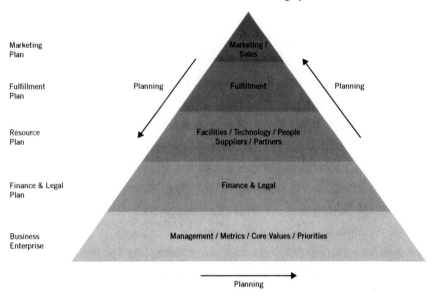

Exhibit Q: Business Planning Pyramid

→ Each step broadens in scope and supports the steps above and across.

→ Plans are developed by sales channel which are uniquely defined based on differing functional process.

- There are five levels to setting a longer-term business strategy: Marketing Plan, Fulfillment Plan, Resource Plan, Financial and Legal Plan, and Business Enterprise Strategy. Each could be different based on the sales channel. Determine what is common and unique for each channel.
- Planning starts with the customer and flows down the functional model, then back up based on supporting resource capabilities, strengths, weaknesses, competitive advantages, and limitations.
- Implementation is managed by establishing themes which support functional strategies and cross functional areas. Then specific actions focusing on improving value factors are defined within themes.

- A matrix planning document can be used to define common and unique processes by sales channel.
- Ultimately, Finance and Legal determines the viability of the model based on financial capabilities and targets and legal considerations.

Always start with the customer and begin to move down the model. For example, who are your ideal customers? What are their demographics and psychographics? Why are they ideal for you? Sales and Marketing will define what is necessary to attract, land, and service the ideal customers. Then Fulfillment can respond by specifying what they need in order to fulfill the needs defined. Next, Operations can respond with what they need to have the product or service ready for Fulfillment. From there, you can define the resources required: people, IT, facilities, and partners. Finally, Finance and Legal can address the monetary and legal requirements.

At this point, you begin to see constraints. A key part of this process is making trade-offs between the functional groups, and between long-term and short-term actions. Finance may respond by saying, "We don't have the money for all that." So the process starts moving the other way, and you need to begin to consider trade-offs. If you can't get the resources that Operations and Fulfillment need to accomplish their goals, will they be able to meet the requirements of Sales and Marketing and the demands of the customer? If not, how do you need to reframe the strategy? What ultimate impact will this have on the customers?

It will force Sales and Marketing to more clearly define what they must have versus what they would like to have. With this knowledge, you can start moving back down the pyramid. You continue with this until the entire organization is in alignment. Finally, once you decide what the game plan is, you set integrated actions in each group, define the most important three to five actions that are critical path, (at the business enterprise level), agree to the management priorities and metrics that will give you feedback on how you are doing, and also have a reality check that these actions are in alignment with your core purpose. This is done from both a business and personal standpoint.

THE WILL TO DO

A plan helps you prioritize, organize, and focus. But at the end of the day, it's still all about the will to execute. Peter Christman once said to me, "There are a lot of people that can do, but not a lot of people that will do." Value Acceleration is how you execute and deliver.

With your core purpose, your core values, your two areas of market domination, your brand, and the three to five competencies that need to be developed defined, you are now in position to turn the vision into reality. With the direction clear, focus on the next year and next quarter. Set one-year and 90-day business and personal goals and priorities. What three to five key actions will you complete in the next year to move the company and your personal planning toward the three- to five-year targets? With these one-year goals set, you can now create an action plan, both personal and business, around three to five key priorities to execute in the next 90 days. These are your "big rocks."

Everyone in business knows, whether we like to admit it or not, that an organization can only realistically focus on a few things at a time. I know there are 30 things that need to be done. But what are the most important five "big rocks" in the next 90 days that must be accomplished to move you toward achieving your one-year goals, which, in turn, will help you build the three to five competencies you need to develop to reach your targets and achieve your vision?

> The *big rocks* analogy comes from a story about a professor who was teaching a group of high-powered, overachieving students about

the importance of setting priorities. During the class, he pulled out a one-gallon, wide-mouthed Mason jar and set it on a table in front of him. Then he produced about a dozen fist-sized rocks and carefully placed them, one at a time, into the jar. When the jar was filled to the top and no more rocks would fit inside, he asked, "Is this jar full?" Everyone in the class said, "Yes." Then he said, "Really?" He reached under the table and pulled out a bucket of gravel. Then he dumped some gravel in and shook the jar, causing pieces of gravel to work themselves down into the spaces between the big rocks.

Then he smiled and asked the group once more, "Is the jar full?" By this time the class was onto him.

"Probably not," one of them answered. "Good!" he replied. And he reached under the table and brought out a bucket of sand. He started dumping the sand in and it went into all the spaces left between the rocks and the gravel. Once more he asked the question, "Is this jar full?"

"No!" the class shouted. Once again he said, "Good!" Then he grabbed a pitcher of water and began to pour it in until the jar was filled to the brim. Then he looked up at the class and asked, "What is the point of this illustration?"

One eager beaver raised his hand and said, "The point is, no matter how full your schedule is, if you try really hard, you can always fit some more things into it!" "No," the professor replied, "that's not the point. The truth is: If you don't put the big rocks in first, you'll never get them in at all."

To focus and execute, you should set no more than five business and five personal actions that can completed in the next 90 days (big rocks). Once you decide what these are, ask who is going to champion the action, who needs to be involved, and what the specific deliverable is.

WORKSHOPS, NOT MEETINGS

> Bossidy wrote, "A contemporary strategic plan must be an action plan."

You don't set actions by having an untold number of "meetings." You need to think in terms of workshops, not meetings. What's the difference? The purpose of a meeting is to communicate information. But often, you don't get much more accomplished than that. A workshop has a deliverable and takes a different tone. In a workshop, which should be timed, you go beyond communicating. You robustly debate. You make decisions. You leave with a set of actions everyone is aligned to.

In a workshop, you gather ideas, write them down, hang them on the wall, and debate and agree on actions to be taken when you leave the room. Having a clear set of actions validates what you want to achieve, but more importantly, because it is based on reality, it indicates what you are likely to achieve. It takes the vision and brings it down to earth.

Your goal should be to complete your workshops in no more than two to three hours. Workshops lose effectiveness if they last more than three hours. People get burned out and their brains turn to mush. In the workshop, focus on three things:

- Avoid information overload
- Get agreement on next steps
- Develop relationships

AVOID INFORMATION OVERLOAD

There will be a lot of information pouring out in these workshops. You can manage this by setting an agenda and time limits. Don't let conversations go on and on. If necessary, keep a side board. If you get stuck on something, write it on the side board so that it can be addressed later. Perhaps schedule a "meeting" after the workshop to find out what all the fuss is about. It may or may not be important to the team. Clearly, the person who brought it up thought it was important, so you should at least address it. But try to keep the group moving toward its workshop deliverable.

GET AGREEMENT ON NEXT STEPS

First, everyone needs to realize that you cover different points of view, but at some point within the time limit of the workshop, you need to agree on the next steps. If the group cannot come to a consensus, the champion of the action has the final decision. As the owner, you may overrule the champions, but be careful. If you find yourself constantly overruling the champion, you probably have the wrong champion or you are a control freak. Both are bad. One of the ways I test myself is by what I call the "50% Rule."

My management team knows that as the owner, I reserve the right to make the final call on priorities. However, if we disagree and I am overruling you more than 50% of the time when we disagree, I probably have the wrong person as the champion or I am over-controlling. It's one or the other. I either have confidence in my staff's decisions or I do not. So, I monitor this. When I disagree with the staff, I ask myself: Have I been overruling them more than 50% of the time? If I am, I need to reflect on why and make a change.

Over the years, this rule has challenged me to trust my staff's decisions. At least 50% of the time, I'll run with their point of view whether I agree with it or not. Of course, I won't let them walk off a cliff. But I am willing to live with a few ill-advised decisions if they learn from them. In fact, this is the best way for them to learn. They are not always right, as they don't have the wisdom and experience that I do. And I realize and accept that I am not always right either. But most of the time, they *are* right and it has allowed me to feel more comfortable not being involved in every decision. This has allowed me more time to work on my business instead of in it. At the same time, it has helped them think more like owners instead of employees, work better as a team, back each other up, and accept the consequences of their decisions.

DEVELOP RELATIONSHIPS

These workshops allow your organization to develop respectful relationships. By respectful, I mean appreciating different points of view. The staff will not always agree because they have different points of view on the same subject. Uncle Freddie, my mentor at Sherwin Williams, called this "functional myopia." Everyone looks at the world from their point of view. Most of the time, there is not a right or wrong answer. The key to effective relationships is to try to open up your mind and see things from other points of view. I call this "stretching the rubber band." Who wants a bunch of people who think like robots? What you want is diverse perspectives and people who are willing to stretch the rubber band and consider solutions from different viewpoints. This is the beauty of having a diverse management team.

THE IMPORTANCE OF ALIGNMENT

Many organizations have the knowledge. But it's applying this knowledge that wins the day. You do this by having a system which integrates the application of knowledge that creates and sustains improvements. Having a great game plan isn't enough. If each member of the team does not act when the play is called, you don't move the ball downfield. Your team needs to be in alignment with the vision and internalize it into what they do every day.

Everyone needs to align with the top three to five priorities. Align your team in workshops, where you develop and set your top five personal and business actions. These workshops provide great learning and teaching opportunities, both from you sharing your wisdom and posing a lot of questions and from the team sharing its various points of view. It helps everyone see the company as a whole and how each functional group within the company fits into it. Your key employees will build relationships based on learning how to prioritize, choose, allocate, and assign resources to complete the action.

They will find this process energizing and their skills and capabilities will develop, which will grow your human capital. You will build customer capital, too, as employees will feel connected to how their actions ultimately affect the customer. It will build structural capital. Your strategy will be connected right down the specific actions that must be completed in the next 90 days and you will be able to specifically document and communicate to your successor the story of how you went from point A to point B. And finally, you will begin to build stronger social capital as your key employees build relationships, build confidence, and expand their capabilities. They will thrive off the energy created from succeeding as a team.

So with that, let me ask you:
- Can your staff articulate your company vision and values?
- Can they state two areas of the market where you want to dominate and proof points demonstrating your commitment to these?
- Have you established clear company and individual Standards of Performance? Does your staff receive regular feedback, including one-year and 90-day goals and objectives for the company and individually? Do you meet regularly to reconnect and recalibrate if necessary?
- Do they feel their individual goals and objectives are in alignment with each other's goals and objectives and the company's?
- Do you have learning and growth goals established (and included in their goals) to encourage them to build their competency? How much have you budgeted for professional development?
- Is there an internalized rhythm in the company that facilitates good communication on a regular basis?
- Is your staff connected with the expected financial performance of the company? Do they understand how their actions affect the company's profitability and value?
- Does your financial incentive system reward staff for creating value?

THE IMPORTANCE OF ACCOUNTABILITY

Years ago, my client's management team was doing a team exercise in which they wanted to associate a quote that described the character of each manager. To my delight, they included me and my quote was, "Is it done?" We all had a good laugh about it.

At every quarterly renewal, I had earned a reputation for asking the simple question, "Is it done?" over and over. The reason I always asked was that I wanted the managers to own accountability. Done is done. You either met the goal or you didn't. Typically, you heard a lot of excuses.

Well, I almost got it done but this came up and that came up and I tried, but couldn't fully complete the task.

Missing the goal could be attributed to any variety of reasons. You didn't define the scope of the task properly. Something unanticipated happened that threw you off course. You didn't get the resources. You made the wrong assumptions. But the bottom line is, you got it done or you didn't. And you need to own that. It's hopefully not the end of the world. You should be exploring the reasons why you did not produce the desired outcome. It doesn't necessarily mean you are a bad person or bad manager. At the end of the day, it didn't get done. You still need to own it.

I will always remember receiving my first "marginal" score on a review from my first real mentor, "Uncle Freddie," at Sherwin Williams. I was a young hard-charger and took a lot of pride in being someone who could be relied on to "get things done." Fred had given me five objectives to complete. At my review, he gave me a marginal rating on one of the five things because I didn't get it done. Fred handed out his review in advance of the meeting with him so you could read it and prepare for the evaluation meeting. I remember being quite upset at seeing "M" next to one of my goals. "I'm not marginal," I remember thinking. At the meeting with Fred, I immediately went into all the reasons that were outside my control that prevented me from achieving the goal.

Fred agreed. There were several things that happened outside of my control that contributed to my inability to get that goal accomplished. So I calmed down and said, "So that means you are going to change the score, right?" He responded, "No, you didn't achieve it, so a marginal score is appropriate." I said, "C'mon, we just agreed that it wasn't in my control."

Fred responded, "Yes, we did agree on that. However, you either met the goal or you didn't. Did you meet the goal?"

"Well no, but, but, but..." Before I could finish, Fred interrupted: "You were responsible and you are accountable. It's that simple. You either accomplished it or you didn't. You missed it, and therefore, I'm giving you a marginal."

Fred continued, "I am not saying you are bad person or a bad manager. In fact, on all the other goals I gave you a High Standard. Overall, you did very well. And your overall rating is High Standard. You are a great manager and are getting better. But for that particular item, you failed. Own it."

Setting goals, making promises, and keeping them are at the heart of accountability. Not only must you commit to the deliverable, but you need to be smart enough about your business obligations to understand how to choose priorities, set goals and objectives, and scope ways in which we are committed to achievement. Accountability is not only about delivering. It's also about setting the scope of promises to be kept.

My most valuable managers are the ones that I can count on to keep promises. When they say they are going to get something done, I can trust that it will be done, and done to the standards that represent our brand. They don't always achieve their goals completely. They make mistakes. They sometimes set goals that are too aggressive because they are high achievers. But they own it. Missing objectives, however, should not be about beating people up, although sometimes that's needed too. Most of the time, it's because you didn't understand your business well enough to make the right choices and commitments. Making or not making objectives is an opportunity to learn. But you need metrics to establish the bar and to be able to quantifiably measure your ability to deliver on promises.

THE IMPORTANCE OF RHYTHM

Every company, like most people, has a rhythm to how it proceeds through the days, weeks, and months. There is a flow in your business. This flow reflects what it is like to work at your company, work with your company (tone and manner), and how you get things done.

Once you have prioritized your actions, aligned your team, and established metrics defining what success means, you need to build habits which reinforce the day in and day out, moment-by-moment routines of actually implementing them—that's execution. These routines need to produce outcomes that demonstrate the team's commitment to completing the prioritized actions. This is where you get into the real nitty-gritty process of actually doing, not just thinking. Accomplishing these actions requires your teams to work well together by communicating regularly, collaborating on their own, creating opportunities to focus not only what needs to get done but when it gets done, the steps to get it done, actually doing it, and producing the outcome.

Vision, alignment, accountability, and rhythm are the foundation for relentless execution. But at the end of the day, you still have to execute. You have to deliver. You have to get things done. Execution is how the game is won. Execution alone can be your competitive advantage. You need a fast and flexible system to facilitate disciplined execution. Value Acceleration is that system. If followed and reinforced, with committed resources, Value Acceleration will produce results. Execution will convert your vision into reality.

SECTION THREE

How to Implement Value Acceleration

In this section, you will learn *how* to implement the Value Acceleration management and life planning system into your daily personal and business life.

CHAPTER NINE

GATE ONE | DISCOVER: The Triggering Event

Let's start the implementation of Value Acceleration by recalling the concept of Master Planning. There are three identified keys (legs) to a successful transition: maximizing the value of the business, ensuring you are personally and financially prepared to maximize net proceeds, and ensuring you have a plan for what you are going to do next.

You Can't Always Get What You Want
The Rolling Stones

No, you can't always get what you want
You can't always get what you want
But if you try sometime you find
You get what you need

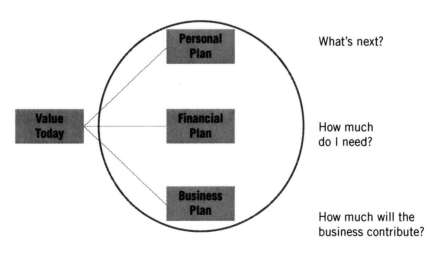

Exhibit R: Master Planning

To move from concepts to action, you need to integrate exit strategy practices into the daily operations of your business. You do that by focusing on creating value using the Five Stages of the Value Maturity and the Value Maturity Index as your guide:

1. Identify Value
2. Protect Value
3. Build Value
4. Harvest Value
5. Manage Value

The first step in the Value Acceleration Methodology is to identify what you already have. This provides a baseline measurement of value going forward, which is needed for business planning, tax and estate planning, and personal planning. This is called the **Triggering Event**.

Exhibit S: The Value Acceleration Methodology

The Triggering Event correlates your business valuation to your personal, financial, and business assessments. All businesses trade in a range of value. Where you sit in that range of value is based on three factors: (1) the results of your financial analysis and benchmarking; (2) your attractiveness score; and (3) your readiness score.

In my experience, owners who complete the Triggering Event feel compelled to go forward with action 70% of the time. You will discover things about your business and your personal aspirations that were not previously evident: things like potential wealth you may be leaving on the table, a greater awareness of your risks, and quantifiable opportunities to grow value.

The Triggering Event gets the whole value growth process going. Why? Because you now have quantitative proof of the value of your business. More importantly, you have a list of specific actions you can take to de-risk and increase the value and transferability of your business. Even if you are considering a transition via an ESOP, management or partner buy-out, or family succession, you have a list of actions that will substantially improve the likelihood of the transition being successful. If you don't want to transfer it at this time, you still have a list of actions that, if implemented, will make your business perform better without you. And should a tragedy strike, you will be ready for that, too.

When people ask me to describe the biggest benefit of completing the Triggering Event, I answer with one word: **clarity**.

For the first time (or the first time in a while), you have a clear view of your business and can make clear choices on what to do next and what those choices mean, in terms of business value and personal wealth. You can quantify the investment needed and the return on value expected as a result of implementing these value growth actions. These returns are worth millions of dollars, and often 10 times or more than your investment. You come away not only understanding the value of your business today, but *how* your business is valued and what you need to do to accelerate that value.

For the advisors reading this book, the Triggering Event is your key to getting owners to realize what they have, to educate them, and to ultimately get them going down the right track. You don't have to "sell" owners on action once they complete the Triggering Event. The opportunities for value acceleration are very clear (if they can be implemented). Implementation routines are covered in Chapter 11, within the PREPARE GATE.

Exhibit T: The Guided Discovery Steps and Deliverables

- ✓ Recast income statement and balance sheet
- ✓ Complete financial analysis
- ✓ Pull benchmarking data
  - Industry performance
  - Recent trade multiples
- ✓ Complete a Personal, Financial, and Business Assessment which scores the business's attractiveness and the owner's personal, financial, and business readiness
- ✓ Correlate the interview scores with the business valuation and financial analysis

Deliverable:
- ✓ A specific and qualified list of personal, financial, and business strengths and weaknesses
- ✓ Correlated and used to justify present value and potential value
- ✓ To establish a dollar value with regard to what value enhancement is worth

Prioritized Action Plan is created
- ✓ Personal / Financial actions
- ✓ Business actions

Which will be implemented in 90-Day "Sprints" (Interval Training)

Let me take a moment here to talk about business valuation. CPAs and certified valuators understand this, but business owners may not. This book is not a book on valuation. Yet it's important that you understand that different valuation methods are used for different purposes.

For this purpose, you are focusing on the strategic value of the business if it were to go to market and be sold to a third party. Knowing what your business is worth today sets the baseline. However, just as important is knowing the business's potential strategic value if you were to improve your value drivers. This goal, along with these value drivers, will be used to set personal and business strategies and tactics to mitigate risks and improve performance. Strategic value represents the gross value if you were to cash in by selling the business. The main purpose of this technique is to educate you about valuation and initiate strategic discussions to clarify what you want to do next from a personal, financial, and business standpoint. It is not the value used for family, employee, partner/management transitions, or estate and tax planning.

THE REAL NUMBER VS. THE TAX NUMBER

Most owners do not have a realistic view of the value of their business and its contribution to their overall net worth. There are two numbers in every business:

- Tax number
- Real number

Your tax number is the number you see on your financial statements every month or quarter (depending on how often you review them). The real number is the cash flow or cash benefit of what your business is really producing. In the professional services industry, it is often referred to as the "normalized" number. It can be much higher than the tax number. Yet, in my experience, it's rare that this number is *ever* presented to the owner, let alone actively managed, until the owner decides to sell.

The normalized number is often expressed as EBITDA (Earnings Before Interest, Taxes, Depreciation, and Amortization). EBITDA is generally accepted as the best number to use to express the cash flow being generated by the business. This is easy enough to calculate. To start, you take your net income and "add back" to it interest, taxes, depreciation, and amortization.

This is closer, but it's still not your "real" number. To determine your real number, often referred to as "Recasted EBITDA," you also need to add back or take away things like one-time, non-recurring expenses; non-customary or non-ordinary salaries with related expenses; discretionary bonuses and pension investments; and other discretionary expenses that you may have chosen to charge to the business, but that the new owner may choose not to.

To get to a recasted number, you adjust any number on the income statement that does not reflect a true picture of the cash flows of the business. These might include things like:

- Sales that were pulled forward or pushed out from one year to the next.
- Any non-recurring, one-time, or out-of-the-ordinary costs and expenses. These might be things like a big bonus that was paid out in one year, a big one-time investment that was expensed rather than capitalized, a large legal settlement, or excessive or under-market salaries and rent.
- "Discretionary" expenses of the owner(s), also known as addbacks, which would include things like having your spouse or children on the payroll when they don't actually work there, expenses related to personal property, a country club membership, a personal car, health care for the owner, or certain insurances that would be considered discretionary like long-term disability. These are things the future buyer of the company could eliminate when you aren't there anymore.
- Standard addbacks include interest, taxes, depreciation, and amortization.

Some owners are very conservative about charging these "discretionary" expenses to the business while others abuse the opportunity. I'm not taking a position on that; it's your business and it's your choice. However, for valuation purposes, you want the EBITDA number to reflect the most likely cash benefit that will be transferred to the new owner. Understanding your "real" number is another benefit of the Triggering Event. Completing this recasting exercise alone can be very educational and revealing.

The difference between your tax number and the real number can be significant, and as such, will have a significant impact on your valuation. A business I worked with several years ago showed net income for one year of $672,000. We were using a multiple of four times EBITDA as the basis for our valuation. Using the $672,000 net income number, this business would have been valued at $2,688,000. However, the owner provided a list of adjustments that totaled $637,000, which raised the Recasted EBITDA to $1,309,000 and the valuation to $5,236,000. That's a difference of $2,548,000, or nearly 95%!

One big problem is that most accounting systems are not built to give owners regular feedback on the "real" number and what can be done to improve it. Again, I'm not suggesting the tax number isn't important. Instead, I believe you need a management system that gives you feedback on both on a regular basis. The first step to accomplish this is to identify what you already have. Then you can initiate steps to mitigate risk, maximize value, and position your business properly so that you can unlock its wealth on any timeline.

STEP 1: FINANCIAL RECASTING

The process of determining your real number versus the tax number is called financial recasting.

The purpose of recasting is to demonstrate a true picture of your company's cash flows and assets, liabilities, and net worth. Both the balance sheet and income statement should be recast, but I suggest you focus on the income statement, since that is what you will use to determine your business value within the Value Acceleration Methodology.

If you are not sure how to pull this set of numbers together, you may want to get the help of a CPA or Value Advisor (CEPA). They will know what to ask, where to look, and will provide you with a list of what to look for and report. Avoiding abuse with regard to this recasted number is important. If you value the business and then try to sell it, a buyer will look very closely at the adjustments made to determine recasted EBITDA.

A synergistic buyer will also look hard to see where synergies can be created. If one of your competitors buys the business, they may be able to reduce facilities and staffing. As the present owner, you will get credit for this. For example, if you are paying yourself $300,000 per year and you can be eliminated after the sale, this amount will be added back, and you will get credit for the $300,000 times whatever your multiple is. So if your business is worth four times EBITDA, eliminating you as the owner, is really worth $1.2 million in value.

DIY FINANCIAL RECASTS

You can recast these numbers yourself. But again, my recommendation is that you get a CPA and CEPA to help you figure this out. After you do the initial recast, you will want to get a regular read on this number. I do this each quarter. It takes some time and expense to set up the first time, but after that, it's very manageable.

I do this for all my businesses and ongoing clients, although this could easily be done by your CPA. I am always amazed how many CPAs don't recast the numbers on a regular basis for their clients. This is really a simple, justifiable, value-added service that they can provide. If you are like me, and I am sure you are, I want my CPA to provide me with useful financial analysis about how my business is performing, not just raw financial data pushed my way. I suggest it all the time, but instead, many of my clients' CPAs choose to send the financial statements to me; I recast and present them to the owner.

DRAWBACKS OF ADDBACKS

Addbacks really need to be managed because they can get excessive. I've seen owners adding back their kids' coaching camps and homeowners' association fees, electric bills, and hundreds of thousands of dollars in personal expenses. It's really staggering sometimes. Grossly excessive addbacks can be a deterrent. If the addbacks are too excessive, it makes the investment banker and buyer very nervous, and sometimes the banks and buyers won't accept all of them. Plus, this is usually a sign that you are undercapitalizing the business, severely hampering the probability of successfully transitioning it to family, employees, or management. If you are abusing addbacks, it means the recasted EBITDA that was used to value your business is then way too high. After being adjusted by the bank or buyer, it will reduce the valuation and, in turn, lessen what a bank would be willing to finance or what a buyer would be willing to pay for your business.

You should note that adjustments go both ways. They are not always in your favor as the owner. For example, if, for some reason, your salary is less than what a CEO of a company your size should be paid or you are under-investing in the business, your expenses could be adjusted up, reducing your recasted EBITDA number.

I saw this a few years ago with a client working through Value Acceleration with the goal to sell to a strategic buyer. Sales were growing significantly. The owner's net income was skyrocketing. But one of the things I noted in my benchmarking analysis was that he was under-investing in the business. I deduced this because his SG&A (Selling, General, and Administration) as a percent to sales was much lower than the industry average. As a result, sales were growing at a much faster rate than costs and expenses. So I asked him about it. He told me it was not intentional.

"The whole company is working so hard to keep up with sales, Chris," he explained. "I haven't had the time to even add the people I need to keep up, let alone make investments in my systems and facilities."

He was sitting on a house of cards. Any buyer looking at the business would see the same thing. So when preparing his recasted income statement and balance sheet, I made adjustments indicating expenses as a percent to sales would increase rather than decrease in the future. This reduced his recasted EBITDA, but produced a realistic, recasted financial statement and corresponding valuation.

After reviewing the business's financial statements, the strategic buyer commented that she was going to have to invest additional funds to sustain the present growth rate. I agreed and was able to show her how we already had planned for that and adjusted the projected financial statements accordingly. This built a lot of credibility with the buyer. It also helped me manage my client's expectations as the seller by painting a more realistic picture of what he could reasonably sell the business for on the open market.

Keep in mind that the balance sheet should be recasted as well. If there is excessive working capital or retained earnings in the business, you might pull that out. Or you might need to clean up intercompany and personal loans and other liabilities. Again, get a CPA or CEPA. Make step one an easy one.

STEP 2: FINANCIAL ANALYSIS AND BENCHMARKING

An owner who doesn't know his numbers doesn't know his business. Once you have your recasted income statement and balance sheet, you must conduct a financial analysis by studying the numbers and trends to prepare a forecast.

In your analysis, benchmark your numbers to similar companies in your industry. How do you stack up? It can be quite revealing. I also believe in keeping it simple. Concentrate on gross margin as a percent to sales and EBITDA as a percent to sales. Simply by looking at these two benchmarks, you will see how you stack up.

If you are underperforming, you won't yet have data as to why, but at least you will know how you measure against your peers and that there is opportunity for improvement. The attractiveness and readiness scoring in the next step will reveal why. You should also compare your numbers to businesses outside your industry to see if there is anything you might learn by looking outside the box.

I have looked at hundreds of companies and financial statements over the years, maybe even thousands. With my experience, I can pick up a ton of information about how a company operates just from studying the recasted financials. This will benefit you, even if you do not actively handle daily operations. If you are not comfortable doing this yourself, get a good, experienced advisor who really understands recasting and can read between the lines of your financial statements. Your CPA or CEPA has these skills.

Additionally, there are groups that can provide you with a part-time CFO, such as Focus CFO and B2B CFO. These are experienced financial people that you probably could not afford to hire full-time, but you could use their services on a fractional basis. They are not accountants, although many have an accounting background. They act more as strategic financial advisors specifically for your business. Again, your business is likely 80% or more of your net worth, so if you don't have these skills, hire someone who does.

STEP 3: DETERMINE THE RANGE OF VALUE

With a clean set of recasted financials and your financial analysis and benchmarking complete, turn your attention to figuring out what the private capital market is willing to pay for companies like yours and calculate your range of value.

First, you need to understand how value is determined. It can appear very complicated when you hear terms like "Discounted Cash Flow" and "Weighted Average Cost of Capital" and technical terms like that. But depending on the purpose of valuation, calculating your business value is actually simple math. And for your purposes, that simple math is all you will need.

The formula for determining the value of your business is not complex. It is "recasted" cash, usually expressed as EBITDA, times a cash market multiple and recasted sales times a sales market multiple. Items on the left side of the equation, cash and sales, are typically under your control. All other things being equal, the more cash, the higher your value. The more sales, the higher your value. That's pretty easy to understand.

Exhibit U: Strategic Value—Simple Math

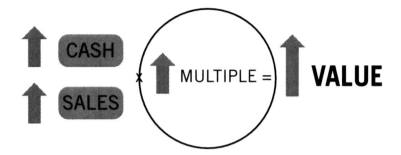

Predictable Cash Flow   Private Capital Market Conditions
Clean Balance Sheet   Terms / Exit Option
Size Matters!   **Intangibles** (Value Factors)

You Control   You Control Some

You probably focus mainly on the left side of the equation: sales and income. But that's a big mistake because the multiple in the center of the equation is really where the game is played and value is accelerated. If you do not recall Chapter 7, The Four C's, where we discussed intangible versus tangible assets and the four types of intellectual capital, stop here. Go back and read it again before continuing.

The multiple range is determined by the private capital market. It can also be influenced by the terms of a deal, the structure of your business, and your exit option choice. The market will take this range up and down depending on the state of the private capital markets, economy, and the industry you are in. You can't control this.

But as I said previously, this multiple has a range. For example, some businesses in your market may trade at three times EBITDA, while others trade at a multiple of eight. Some businesses may trade at 50% of sales and others trade at 100% or more.

This difference will have a significant impact on your valuation. For example, let's suppose you have a recasted EBITDA of $2 million. If you trade at four × EBITDA, your valuation would be $8 million. But if you traded at seven × your valuation at the same EBITDA level, it would be $14 million, 75% higher. So what factors earn you a high or low multiple?

These are the intangibles, and you, as the owner, can control these. You cannot control the range, but you *can* control where you land in the range. Your position will depend on the strength of your intellectual capital, which you can quantitatively measure using the attractiveness and readiness scores.

Where do you get this comparable data? There are several data options available. I use a product called *Pratt's Stats* as one primary resource. Pratt's Stats is a database of financial information related to companies that have sold. Typically, the investment banker who handled the deal anonymously posts financial data related to the company. For a reasonable annual fee, you can get access to this data, download it, and review it. Now, just like any other database, you need to scrub it. It takes some skill and experience to scrub the data. But there are many other resources available as well. I have a list and descriptions of them on my site (www.SniderValueIndex.com). I use a variety of them and compare the information I get from each, looking for consistent and inconsistent patterns to make sure I am comfortable with the accuracy of the data and what it is revealing to me.

In the example below, I chose and plotted 12 companies that were reasonable comparables to one of my client's businesses:

Exhibit V: Industry Multiples Comparables

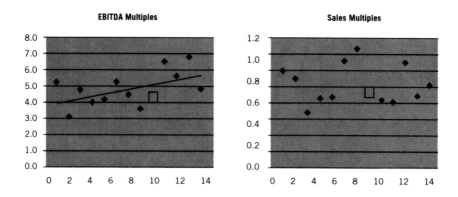

The EBITDA multiples ranged from a low of just over 3.0 to a high of just under 7.0 with a median of 4.8. The sales multiples ranged from a low of around 50% to sales to high of around 110% of sales and had a median of 69%. After plotting them, enter the low, median, and high into a worksheet (see below). Calculate the midpoints between each of these. For example, the midpoint between 50% and 69% is 60%. Now you have the range of multiples in your industry.

Industry Multiples

	Low		Median		High
Sales Multiplier	50%	60%	69%	90%	110%
EBITDA Multiplier	3.10	3.95	4.80	5.85	6.90

Using the mathematical formula (CASH + SALES × MULTIPLE = VALUE), you can do some simple math to calculate your range of value. Pull your trailing 12 months (TTM) recasted sales and recasted EBITDA information from Step 1. For illustration purposes, I will use $10,500,000 in recasted sales and $1,300,000 in recasted EBITDA (see below).

	Amount
TTM Recasted Sales:	$10,500,000
Recasted TTM EBITDA:	$1,300,000
EBITDA % to Sales:	12.38%

Now do the math (see below).

Range of Value

	Low		Mid-Point		High
Sales mult:	$5,250,000	$6,037,500	$6,825,000	$9,187,500	$11,550,000
EBITDA mult:	$4,030,000	$5,135,000	$6,240,000	$7,605,000	$8,970,000
Average:	$4,640,000	$5,586,250	$6,532,500	$8,396,250	$10,260,000

The range of value using the sales multiple method is $5,250,000 to $11,550,000, with a median of $6,825,000. The range of value using the EBITDA multiple is $4,030,000 to $8,970,000 with a median of $6,240,000. Combining the two produces an average range of $4,640,000 to $10,260,000 with a median of $6,532,500. You have now produced 15 valuation points ranging from roughly $4.0 million on the low end to $11.5 million on the high end. This is your range of value.

There are a few things you might notice right away from this analysis. First, the range is quite large. The high end ($11.5 million) is almost triple the low end ($4.0 million). That is not unusual. It reflects the difference in value of discount companies versus best-in-class companies.

Second, you will notice the differences in the values using the EBITDA multiple versus the sales multiple. In the example above, the midpoint using the sales method is $6.8 million, versus the EBITDA midpoint method at $6.2 million. This is your first benchmark.

If your value using EBITDA is less than your value using sales, it tends to indicate that you are underperforming financially compared to similar companies in your industry. One of the ways you can double-check this is by going back to your sample and calculating the average and median EBITDA as a percent to sales. You can look at what the best-in-class companies have been producing (I put these at the top 20%) and what the average of all companies are producing.

In my sample, the average EBITDA as a percent to sales was 13.60% and the best-in-class were in the range of 15.80%. If you multiply these percentages by your TTM sales, you produce a theoretical average and best-in-class recasted EBITDA benchmark (see below).

	Amount	Average	BIC
TTM Sales:	$10,500,000		
Adjusted TTM EBITDA:	$1,300,00	$1,428,000	$1,659,000
EBITDA % to Sales:	12.38%	13.60%	15.80%

You can interpret this to mean that if your company was an average performer, you would be producing $1,428,000 in recasted EBITDA versus your actual $1,300,000 at $10,500,000 in sales. This difference is $128,000 (or about 10%). It reflects how much more cash flow your business could be generating for you if it were operating at average. In this case, it implies that your business is a below-average performer.

Exhibit W: Profit Gap

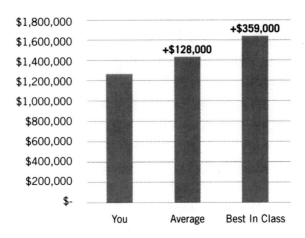

If you were operating in the top 20%, among the best-in-class, you would be generating 15.80% EBITDA to sales or $1,659,000 in recasted EBITDA. This is $359,000 more cash annually (or nearly 27%). These two variances represent the Profit Gap. Combined, they demonstrate how much profit you might be leaving on the table each year because you are not performing as well as you could. This is a Value Acceleration opportunity. But why are you underperforming? Move to the next step and conduct a personal, financial, and business assessment to find out.

STEP 4: PERSONAL, FINANCIAL, AND BUSINESS ASSESSMENT

With your financial analysis complete, you know your range of value and how your financial performance benchmarks against other companies like yours in your industry. You can use this to determine where you land in the range of value, as we saw above.

Keeping to the core principle of personal, financial, and business balance, you can determine why you place where you do by completing a personal, financial, and business assessment. I use a software tool called MAUS, which was developed by my good Australian mate Peter Hickey, CEPA, a self-made businessman and entrepreneur. I like the simplicity of his product. And to me, the simpler, the better. I use two of his indexes: The Business Attractiveness Index and The Readiness Index.

RESOURCES FOR COMPLETING YOUR ASSESSMENT

One of the beautiful things to happen in the industry over the last five years has been the development and release of software products to help conduct these assessments. Several CEPAs have developed their own tools and some are using the tools provided by EPI. The choice of which product to use to evaluate your business is a personal and process preference. One thing I learned in all those years I was implementing software solutions is that software is only a tool. Software doesn't solve problems; people do. It is really much more about how the software is deployed, the processes that surround it, and the users using it.

I recommend that you use a Certified Exit Planning Advisor (CEPA) to conduct the personal, financial, and business assessment with you. You might think I am being self-serving (since I own the Exit Planning Institute and I am a CEPA). But you're wrong. I simply know how critical it is to have the right people in the right seats on your Value Acceleration Bus and I am not one to hold back a solid recommendation. CEPAs are trained and experienced in how to deliver this assessment. They have had to study and pass an exam. They manage this process as their career. And they already utilize the Value Acceleration Methodology with owners on a regular basis.

The assessment involves interviews. I have completed dozens of these over the last several years. I do them for my own businesses and I act as a facilitator to help other business owners complete their assessments. Having someone skilled at conducting this type of interview is extremely helpful. They can answer your questions and clarify what is meant or how you should score. Even more critical, they will challenge some of your answers, asking you why you scored an area this way or that. They will take notes so that they can follow up on some of your answers later, among many, many more benefits that come with having a skilled practitioner. However, if you decide to do it on your own, you should strongly consider purchasing a product like MAUS.

CONDUCTING ASSESSMENT INTERVIEWS

The first time you do an assessment, it is most effective to do so privately, in a one-on-one session with your CEPA. I know there are those who disagree with me on this. They talk about being open and more transparent. But in my opinion, this interview experience is deeply personal, especially the first time you go through it. I feel most owners are more comfortable sharing their true feelings and scoring themselves honestly in a private session than in a group setting.

The time to involve the whole group in a discussion will come later. If you have multiple partners or multiple family members who are owners with you, or you want to involve your management team, I still feel it is best to do individual one-on-one interviews. It takes more time and money to do it this way, but in the end you will get a more honest result. The point of the Triggering Event is to get a clear view of your business, so honesty is not a luxury; it is essential.

Some people are intimidated in a group session, especially if they are going to give a poor score on a value factor that someone else is responsible. If the other person is in the room, they may soften their criticism. You don't want them to soften it. You are the owner; you want the truth.

In addition, with each party responding separately, you are able to determine where the points of view are out of alignment. For example, one person thinks marketing is a 5, best-in-class, and the other thinks it's a 3, slightly below average. That's probably something the partners or management team should have an in-depth conversation about.

However, if these respondents were together while completing the assessment interview, each would be more likely to compromise, perhaps agree to disagree, and settle on a 4 with no further discussion. The reality is, one partner saw it as below average, and the other saw best-in-class for a reason. By agreeing to split the scoring difference, you are avoiding a really great opportunity to get the real picture and get on the same page.

Compromise on the assessment defeats the purpose, don't you think? Brutal honesty, even if tainted, is vital to the process. Also, in order to get the assessment completed in three hours or less, you don't have a lot of time to go in-depth on any one point. Groups want to discuss and debate. You aren't trying to solve problems here, just identify where they exist.

Conducting separate interviews produces interesting variations in perception that are usually important for the partnership to discuss. In fact, this assessment process is a great tool for focusing discussion when partners and family members are not on the same page. Even in my own businesses, I have used the process numerous times assist in resolving family and partner disputes. No matter how much you might try to hide it, a dispute with a partner or in the family permeates the organization. It kills the culture and eventually erodes the performance of the business like a cancer. One of the worst things that can happen in a dispute is for the parties to stop talking to each other.

You can use this process to open up communication and get the partners focused on specific areas of the business, where their points of view are different. The same applies in getting family members, management teams, and boards of advisors to communicate. These different points of view are healthy if managed well, though they can be the source of problems. If nothing else, the process keeps the dialogue going, which often combats the bigger problem of having people stop talking to each other. You can use the process in family situations, where multiple family members are in management roles within the business, or include your management team if you are a larger middle market business.

Although I do not recommend doing so the first time through, you can do this assessment in a workshop format with all needed parties present. This is more time-efficient overall, although it can take one day to several days to get through because consensus needs to be reached for each value factor, as opposed to collecting the scores individually and later discussing major scoring variances.

You should use the option you feel most comfortable with, because when you get to the Prepare Gate, the Value Acceleration Methodology frequently revisits the scores. There are no long-term commitments being made at this point.

COMPLETING THE PERSONAL, FINANCIAL, AND BUSINESS ASSESSMENT

The scoring was discussed earlier, but let's go through it again. Scoring for each value factor ranges from 1 to 6, with 1 being the lowest and 6 being the highest (best-in-class). You never use decimals, so you can't score something 3.5. You need to choose 3 or 4. The best way to score is to start in the middle and then work your way left or right. A score of 3 means you are slightly below average. A 4 means you are slightly above average. Remember, you can't be average. Forcing yourself to choose will help you really think about your performance, which is what I want you to do.

If you think you are best-in-class, meaning you are in the top 20%, then score yourself a 5 or 6. Note: I rarely give out a 6. Hold that rating for something that no one else has...something very, very special. Start by giving yourself a 5 and save the 6s for really special things. 6s should hardly ever be given.

If you've given no thought or effort to something, give yourself a 1 or 2. Use 1s the same way you use 6s: sparingly. Most of the time, you will score yourself between 2 and 4. Even though 2 is far less than average, you will realize as you go through the process just how many things are missing or you have not thought about. You can't score something with a 3 if it does not exist. A 3 means it exists and it's just not that good. But it still exists.

If something is missing or you have not thought about it, you should score yourself a 2 at best. If it's missing and because it is missing, it is really hurting you or your business, score it a 1. If you have something, but its current condition is below average, give yourself a 3. If you have something and you think it's above average, score a 4. If you have something and you really think it's the best out there, better than 80% of any others, give yourself a 5. Give yourself a 6 if you know, meaning you have proof, that no one else has this. Got it?

So if I asked you to score your level of personal planning on a scale of 1 to 6, how would you score?
- If you have done no personal planning at all, score yourself a 1.
- If you have thought about it, but don't have a written plan, give yourself a 2.
- If you have a written plan, but it has not been visited in over a year, perhaps a 3 is right.
- If you have a written plan and it's been updated in the last year, you regularly review it, and have shared it with loved ones, give yourself a 4.
- If you have a written plan, it's been updated in the last year, you regularly review it, you have reviewed it with loved ones and you've built a contingency plan for it, invested in it, and it's tightly integrated with your financial and business planning, give yourself a 5.

Through this process, you will be producing two scores: Business Attractiveness and Exit Readiness. You will be self-scoring, so be honest. If you have a CEPA facilitate, he or she will likely challenge some of your answers. If your CEPA is too kind to challenge you, you might want to consider getting someone who will. Or you need to challenge yourself. After all, this is your life and you're the leader of the team.

Business Attractiveness answers the question "How attractive is your business from an outsider's point of view," meaning in the eyes of a buyer. But understand a "buyer" could be a family member, a partner, or an employee, not just a third-party strategic buyer. There are specific questions related to a strategic buyer, because if maximizing price is your primary goal, selling to a strategic buyer is likely to be your best bet. Bear in mind that a strategic buyer is not just a competitor or member of your company's value chain. Private equity firms and family offices may also be strategic if they are looking at buying you as an add-on to an existing platform company.

The attractiveness index has 25 questions in four categories. You receive a score in each category, and then these are averaged to come up with an overall "Attractiveness Score." A score of 58% is the midpoint, meaning average. A score of 50% or lower is a red flag and indicates a discounted company. A score of 72% or better is considered a premium or best-in-class.

If you score somewhere above 58 but below 72, your business would be considered above average in attractiveness. If you score 50% or lower, it likely means your business is unsalable or unlikely to successfully transition to family, employees, management, or partners. If it can be sold, you would have to provide a substantial discount to encourage a buyer to go forward. I suggest 67% be the target goal, or what I call the Green Zone. A score of 67% means you are above average, but not quite at the best-in-class level. That's still pretty good.

The second index is Exit Readiness. This index asks the question, "How ready are you and the business to transition?" There are 121 questions in 22 personal, financial, and business categories. You will go through the same scoring process as with attractiveness, scoring yourself from 1 to 6. You will receive an average score for each of the 22 categories and then an overall average score for the index.

Exhibit X: Exit Readiness Scorecard

EXIT READINESS SCORE

Government Grants	N/A	N/A	R&D, fed, state, local
Compliance Issues	83%	Premier	Taxes, environment, regulatory, retirement
Systems Processes and Databases	79%	Premier	CRM, accounting, customer, sales
Brand Issues	70%	Meets Goal	Does the brand add value?
Valuation Expectations	70%	Meets Goal	Value and timeframe
Expense Reduction	69%	Meets Goal	SGA, insurance, banking, cash, payroll, GM
Immediate Value Readiness	69%	Meets Goal	How ready right now — strategic buyer?
Personal Knowledge	67%	Meets Goal	Understanding of how buyers place value
Financials	64%	Below Goal	Taxes, management reports, customer analysis
Revenue Drivers	60%	Below Goal	S&M, lead generation, conversion, conversion rate
Product and Marketing Strategies	58%	Below Goal	Product and market strategy analysis
Employee and Management Issues	57%	Below Goal	Reliance, competency, morale, P&P, turnover
Personal Expectations	57%	Below Goal	Post-sale expectations
Customer Contracts	56%	Below Goal	Customers & strategic alliances, warranties, maint
Expense Contracts	50%	Discount	Suppliers, leases, insurance, web, etc.
Marketing Documentation and Systems	50%	Discount	Systematic, proof
Payment Considerations	50%	Discount	Taxes, bonuses, terms, etc.
Credibility and Justification	47%	Discount	Customers, awards, community
Shareholder Goals	44%	Discount	Shareholder alignment, when, how, who
Intellectual Property	42%	Discount	Trademarks, patents, software, domains
Management Systems and Forecasts	39%	Discount	12 months – three years, scorecard
Company Documentation	38%	Discount	Paperwork, operating agreement, buy-sell
OVERALL SCORE	**57%**	**Below Goal**	

GREEN ZONE = 67%+

PREMIUM: 72%+   MID: 51%–72%   DISCOUNT: 50% OR LESS

ATTRACTIVENESS AND READINESS—NOT THE SAME THING

Attractiveness and readiness are not the same thing. Just because your business looks attractive does not mean that it is ready, or that you are personally ready to transition it. Attractiveness is how the business looks from the outside in. Readiness is what's inside.

Consider a good-looking car. It looks beautiful from the outside. Shiny. Nice color. Great wheels. Based on your view of it, your expectation is "this is a really nice car." Now hop inside. The interior is a mess. Look under the hood. Didn't you expect a much bigger engine?

Why does it matter? What typically happens is that someone from the outside looks at your business and it looks attractive, so they make an offer to buy it. At the time of the offer, they have only limited information—probably information you have presented in the best light possible. Then, once they look under the hood, sit down at the wheel, and test drive it, they are disappointed. It looked good from the outside (attractiveness), but once they looked deeper, it did not meet their expectations (readiness). Readiness is just as important as attractiveness, and I could argue, that it is even more important because it also includes personal and financial readiness.

THE UGLY BABY SYNDROME

Business attractiveness and exit readiness are a state of fact, not a state of mind. As owners, we tend to look at our business attractiveness and personal, financial, and business readiness through rose-colored glasses. As a result, you tend to overstate the value of your business. In fact, in a survey by the Alliance of Merger & Acquisition Advisors (AM&AA), 95% of M&A advisors indicated an owner's perception of value compared to its real value is the number one factor why businesses don't sell. The attractiveness index and readiness index provide concrete data to justify your market value and calibrate your expectations.

Andy Kuhar is a friend of mine with extensive experience in buying, selling, and running businesses. He has operated as a CFO and COO for a number of companies and high net worth investors, and has worked in the private equity industry. He has a way of dealing with difficult matters in a humorous way, which is one reason I have him on my board. Andy uses an analogy called the "Ugly Baby Syndrome" to illustrate the misalignment between what an owner thinks the business is worth versus what it is really worth.

Many of you reading this are mothers or fathers. To illustrate the point, suppose we met and you were describing your daughter to me. After you finished telling me how proud you are of her (your baby) and how beautiful she is, I asked you to show me a picture. You eagerly got out a picture, and upon looking at it, I said, "Wow, she is really ugly!" You would probably punch me in the nose. At minimum, you would be very offended. It may be true that she is ugly, but she is still *your* Ugly Baby. That's what it's like when someone looks at your business from the outside in and tells you it is unattractive. It may be true. Your business may be ugly. But it's still your Ugly Baby.

If you achieve a decent score on attractiveness but a lower score on readiness, you still have issues that will lower your valuation. Oftentimes, nice offers come in during the "Letter of Intent" phase, and then get reduced as the buyers complete their due diligence and find issues. Someone is criticizing your Ugly Baby and you take it personally. You get really upset about it, and the deal never closes because you back out (because you were offended). You make excuses to justify backing out of the deal, saying things like the buyer "offended" you or "I don't like his tone," among many others I have heard throughout the years. Or maybe, because you are not ready personally or financially and the business is not ready, you get cold feet five, six, or seven months into the deal. So much time and money wasted. This is common and its why investment bankers have break clauses in their contracts.

You have a bad experience. Whoever is trying to take over your business has a bad experience. Everyone loses money and leaves with a bad taste in their mouth about the process. But the only problem with the process was that it wasn't started soon enough to get you and your business "ready." Thus, when the time came, you couldn't march right through the deal process, educated, and achieve a premium exit price.

Let's be honest. If you have tried this and got a bad result, shame on you. It's your business and your life. If you turn your biggest asset over to a group of advisors or managers who don't know what they are doing, shame on you. If you let them make decisions for you or take over your life's work...shame on you. If you try to transition a business that isn't ready, good luck. You are likely to be in that category of 80% of the businesses that don't sell, or 70% that don't transition to the next generation, or 75% who profoundly regret the decision within a year after exiting. Is that the legacy you want to leave? Of course not.

There are three things you need to consider in honestly completing the attractiveness and readiness assessments:

- First, how attractive is the business from an outsider's point of view?
- Second, is the business ready?
- Third, are you ready?

You need to assess both attractiveness and personal, financial, and business readiness from a state of fact, not a state of mind. You need to be brutally honest. You accomplish this by scoring yourself honestly on each of the 146 value factor questions (25 Attractiveness; 121 Readiness). Then you add these up to determine an overall score in both attractiveness and readiness. The Triggering Event is the process of taking off your rose-colored glasses and embracing the realities, and associated potential, of your business as it is today.

COMMON READINESS ISSUES

The number of different potential readiness issues are numerous. Below are just a few of the more typical issues you might have:

Typical Personal Readiness Issues:
- No owner goals and objectives
- No owner consideration to "What Next?"
- No advisory board or formal transition team
- No contingency plans
- Dated buy-sell agreement
- Shareholders and/or family members not on the same page
- Forced generational transfer
- Failure to mitigate personal risks
- Health issues

Typical Financial Readiness Issues:
- Income requirements post-transition (i.e. standard of living adjustment needed?)
- Needs vs. wants not identified
- Financial plan does not consider the value of the business or has an outdated, overstated, or understated opinion of value
- Net proceeds analysis: what you keep is what matters most
- Tax and estate planning not started soon enough
- No risk sensitivity analysis and profile
- Inappropriate portfolio allocation
- Financial plan not aligned with personal plan and business plan

Typical Business Readiness Issues:
- Missing, outdated (> one year), overstated, or understated valuation
- Stated EBITDA inaccurate—not recasted or not recasted properly
- Multiplier not adequately adjusted for risk, such as customer concentration or branding
- Business is not bankable
- Problematic credibility of financial information: lack of audit, review, compilation of financial statements
- Availability of interim information
- Forecasting (basis, accuracy, assumptions)
- Management/key employee retention
- Have not addressed management succession: will key employees stay on?
- Threat of losing key people: is tribal knowledge retained?
- Customer concentration, meaning one customer accounts for more than 25% of total sales
- Ownership group at odds
- Fishing for an unrealistic price

DEAL KILLERS

Deal killers are easy to identify by a third party. They include things like:
- Owner dependence
- Lack of documentation
- Lack of transferable systems and processes
- Product liability
- EPA/safety issues
- Lawsuits

These are just a sample of some of the many possible personal, financial, and business readiness issues I frequently see during an assessment. If you are not quite ready to bring in a CEPA or purchase assessment software, you can go to my website (www.SniderValueIndex.com) and download a tool called the 54 Value Factors. You can use that to develop a preliminary score on readiness. Another tool you can use is my *Are You Ready? 10 Things To Determine If You Are* (found in Chapter 12). I created "Are You Ready?" prior to designing the *State of Owner Readiness Survey*.

STEP 5: THE TRIGGERING EVENT DELIVERABLE—CORRELATING READINESS TO RANGE OF VALUE

Using your attractiveness and readiness scores, benchmarking data, and financial analysis, you can now objectively and quantitatively support placing your business in the appropriate range of value. If your scores are below average, you would place yourself in the lower end of the range of value, and in the higher end of the range if your scores are above average.

In addition to being able to justify your placement in the range of value, you also have a list (comprising all the items where you scored below 4) of all the actions you can take to begin to drive your placement in the range of value higher, thus achieving a higher valuation. As your score *increases,* your placement in the range of value *increases,* and as a result, your value *increases.*

In the earlier example, I stated the range of value was roughly $4.0 million on the low end to $11.5 million on the high end. I recommend you use the average of the two methods to tighten up the range a bit to $4.6 million on the low end and $10.3 million on the high end. A 58% score (the midpoint) would put you right in the center of the range, at around $6.5 million. A score of 50% to 58% (below average) would assign you around a $5.6 million valuation. A score below 50% (red zone) would place you at around $4.6 million.

Going the other direction on the range of value, a score of 58% to 67% would assign you a valuation of around $8.4 million. If you were best-in-class, represented by a score of 72% or above, it would place you in the highest range at $10.3 million.

Next, double-check your scores against your company's financial performance and benchmarking. Usually there is a direct correlation between financial performance and your scores. In other words, if you scored poorly, it is likely that your financial performance as benchmarked against others in your industry is poor as well. In our example, this business was financially performing below average. Its EBITDA percent to sales was only 12.38% compared to the sample average of 13.6%, and the best-in-class companies are doing 15.8% EBITDA to sales. This makes sense given that the company's attractiveness and readiness scores were below average.

	Amount	Average	BIC
TTM Sales:	$10,500,000		
Adjusted TTM EBITDA:	$1,300,00	$1,428,000	$1,659,000
EBITDA % to Sales:	12.38%	13.60%	15.80%

If you find that you are scoring high and your financial benchmarks are low, it is likely that you have not been honest in your scoring. If this is the case, challenge yourself to be more honest. Not too long ago, I had this exact situation with a client.

> The business was owned by two partners. Tom was a proud, machismo owner who outperformed in all areas, a natural salesman and visionary entrepreneur. Helen, the second owner, provided great balance in ownership to Tom, with complementary skills

and a knack for making the vision touch the ground. As leaders and operators of the business, they had produced some concrete results and certainly took a lot of pride in that.

The owners scored themselves 56% (slightly below average) on their readiness score and 65% (above average) on their attractiveness score. They did have an attractive business, but they were clearly not ready to transition it. They were not ready personally, either.

When I benchmarked their financial performance, they were producing around 9% EBITDA to sales and the industry on average was more like 15%. They were well below average when it came to financial benchmarking, but their self-scores were near average or above average. I challenged them at the workshop to present the results of their Triggering Event, suggesting this didn't make sense.

"I'm questioning if you were really honest when I interviewed you to establish your score because your score was average, but your benchmark was below average."

"Well, it's possible that I rounded up in some areas," Tom confessed.

Across the table, Helen sighed and rolled her eyes at him.

They sat back for bit and then admitted they had probably given themselves higher scores than they should have. In recognizing this disparity, we identified a Value Acceleration opportunity, so we agreed to add an action to look at their SG&A expenses to see if there was money we could save there.

To wrap this up, for the example we have been using, the owner and I eventually settled on a range of value of $5.5 million to $6.5 million. We justified this because:

- The business recasted EBITDA percent to sales was below average
- The Attractiveness Score was above average
- The Readiness Score was slightly below average

When it comes to self-scoring, take off your rose-colored glasses, swallow your pride, and get real with yourself. Don't waste your time—or anyone else's.

THE VALUE GAP

In addition to having a supportable justification for where you place in the range of value, the Triggering Event has more significant benefit in that you will now have a specific list of areas that are holding your valuation down. What are these value factor improvements worth?

As I previously pointed out, if the company in our example was operating at best-in-class level, we could suggest a valuation of $10.3 million. But that is not entirely correct because I used its current recasted EBITDA ($1,300,000) and the current sales ($10,500,000) and the highest multiples in the range of multiples (sales = 110%; EBITDA 6.9) to determine that value. If this business were producing EBITDA at the best-in-class level at $10.5 million in sales, it would have been producing an additional $359,000 in annual EBITDA (refer to Exhibit W: Profit Gap on page 152). So, to get a more accurate read of the value at the best-in-class level, you should be multiplying the best-in-class recasted EBITDA of $1,659,000 and the best-in-class multiple of 6.9. This produces a high-end valuation of $11,447,000 (refer to Exhibit Y: Range of Value on page 169).

Improving both your cash flow and your higher placement in the range of multiples produces an exponential effect on value. With that, you can determine your Value Gap (refer below to Exhibit Z: Value Gap). The Value Gap is the difference between your maximum value in the range ($11,447,100) versus where you actually place ($5,586,250) based on your present scores and benchmarks. This is more than double the present value of the business! And that's what Value Acceleration is worth.

Exhibit Y: Range of Value

	Low		Midpoint		High
Sales mult:	$5,250,000	$6,037,500	$6,825,000	$9,187,500	$11,550,000
EBITDA mult:	$4,030,000	$5,135,000	$6,240,000	$7,605,000	$8,970,000
Average:	$4,640,000	$5,586,250	$6,532,500	$8,396,250	$10,260,000
Benchmarks:		@ 13.6% =	$6,854,400	@ 15.8 =	$11,447,100

Exhibit Z: Value Gap

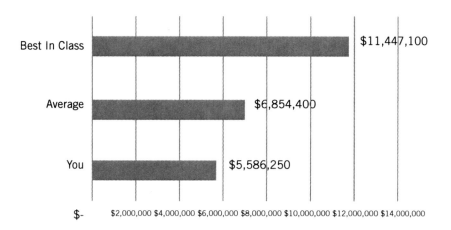

Exhibit AA: Value Growth Opportunity

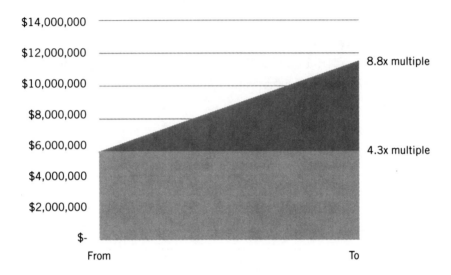

Now, I recognize some professional valuators may have an issue with the way we did this. Some may suggest it's not "scientific enough." You are not looking to be scientific. You will not use this value for estate planning or tax purposes. All you want right now is to get a sense of the strategic range of value for your business, to have some basis for strategic discussion, and an idea of the potential value you could achieve if you invest time and money toward implementing value enhancements.

I am very confident that, given the information from this analysis, this business would sell between $5.5 and $6.5 million. In addition, I am also very confident telling you right now that value enhancement, in this particular case, is worth at least $2.0 to $3.0 million or more... pretty significant. If you focus on Value Acceleration to get both your readiness and attractiveness scores to 67% or higher, it is likely to result in an improvement of your EBITDA as a percent to sales, meaning your cash flow will improve for each dollar of sales you add, and you would be able to sell this business for at least $8.4 million, rather than $5.5 to $6.5 million. Most of us would be willing put $100 on black to see if we could achieve that.

Your next question should be, "How do I protect what I already have?" (in this case, around $5.6 million, which is not $11.5 million, but still a lot of money). Your second question should be, "What do I need to do to move from a valuation of $5.6 million to $11.5 million, and achieve a value improvement of 105%?"

Question #2 has an easy answer. You go back to your attractiveness and readiness scores and look for any value factor that you scored below 4. These are your weaknesses. They're holding your value down. You also want to look at any factor where you scored 4 or above. These are your strengths. You need to leverage these.

This could be a huge list. Your next major step is to build an action plan, which is connected to your long-term vision. You will need to prioritize these actions and assign them to your core and extended teams. You will group these into themes and align your team so that they are all rowing in the same direction. You will establish a set of metrics to measure progress, keep score, and watch your value grow as you successfully implement these actions. And finally, you will use Value Acceleration to build growth mindset routines into your daily personal and business rhythm. Growing value needs to become second nature to you and your teams.

So you know your score. You understand your range of value and where you place. You even know why you sit where you sit. You now have this big list of stuff that, if you can execute, will grow your value. Time to take a look at how to prioritize this list and develop the actions that will get you where you want to be: attractive and ready.

CHAPTER TEN

GATE ONE | DISCOVER: Creating Action Plans

You have completed the Triggering Event. You understand how businesses are valued; the strengths and weaknesses of your personal, financial, and business value factors; and how your score impacts where you land in the range of value. You have completed the first stage of the Value Maturity Index (Identify Value), and as a result, you know what your business is worth today. And you now know what Value Acceleration is worth, outlined in your value gap (remember: the value gap is the quantified dollar value of the difference between your present value and the value of similar best-in-class businesses in your industry).

Exhibit S: The Value Acceleration Methodology

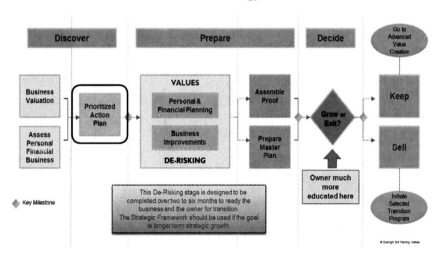

In the Value Acceleration Methodology, you are still in Gate One. Before you pass through the gate, you need to sort through all these actions, and ultimately make a 90-day action plan to get you and your teams deliberately working on value growth. You need a Prioritized Action Plan. You are going to use workshops rather than meetings to prioritize which actions to implement and to measure your progress.

Let's Work Together
Canned Heat/Wilbert Harrison

Together we will stand,
divided we'll fall
Come on now people,
let's get on the ball
And work together, come on, come on
let's work together
Because together we will stand,
Every boy, girl, woman, and man

In my opinion, this is where a lot of the literature on the subject of maximizing value and many of the tools fall short. I have found that owners inherently know what needs to be done to improve the business. That's not the problem. The more common issue is that you lack the discipline to execute, primarily because you don't have a streamlined strategy to deploy. You need a system to actually execute the personal and business changes to protect what you already have, build value, and position yourself to harvest the wealth when that day comes.

I suggest you view Value Acceleration as a management and life planning system. It is a tool to help focus your personal and business teams on value, and guide them through the daily operations of the business and your life. At this point, you may ask, "I already have a management system. What do I need another one for?"

Easy answer. Odds are your present business system (if you have one) does not focus on value. More likely, your management tactics focuses heavily, if not exclusively, on income. I am not suggesting you have to implement a whole new management system. Instead, you need to only make tweaks to your present system so that it drives value *and* income. To accomplish this, your culture will need to change. Your core and extended teams, both personal and business, will need to learn, practice, and test these new concepts for Value Acceleration to be truly internalized.

You, as the owner, need to stay committed. That said, it will be difficult. But it will be worth it. Craig West, an Australian CEPA, uses something he calls the "Wow Curve" to set expectations with his clients. The Wow Curve tracks the team's enthusiasm as you begin the process of implementing actions. What usually happens is that you will come out of the Triggering Event very excited and with a lot of energy. From that point forward, the enthusiasm begins to wane. About nine months later, your Wow factor is at its lowest point.

Why the decline? It's because in the beginning, everyone is excited to get going, but then reality sets in. Change is very difficult and can be as frustrating as it is exciting. Early in the implementation cycles, you will be implementing actions that primarily mitigate risk. This second stage of Value Maturity (Protect Value) is focused on de-risking. These actions are fairly easy to accomplish and you bank some early wins.

But as you progress past the Protect Value stage into the Build Value stage, the changes become more difficult to implement. You will begin working on efficiency improvements and growth initiatives, which means people will need to change the way they do things. Few people like change. This can get a little frustrating for you and for your teams.

If you can get past that inflection point, you are good to go. But you will need commitment to power through this period. Once you are through the thick of it, it's like the lights just came on. One day, everything simply seems to start working. Your culture will begin to change. People will stop viewing these actions as isolated changes and internalize them as "this is the way we do business here." As an owner, it is incredible to watch your business evolve so deliberately. To get there, it will take resolve on your part. Just realize that. Get yourself ready for the challenge.

Growth is really tough and exhausting. It requires you take on change and risk. For this reason, some owners realize that they just don't have the enthusiasm and grit for it anymore, deciding it's time to exit. Others get reinvigorated and find passion for the business again. The beauty of Value Acceleration is that you assess this "Keep or Sell" decision every 90 days. You just take it 90 days at time.

How do you integrate change into your daily company rhythm? The next two chapters are likely the most important chapters in this book because this is where the rubber meets the road. Unless we change what we are doing, unless we execute, even the best strategy will fail. Failure to execute is the biggest threat to your exit strategy. Change must be part of who you are, and the very chemistry of your daily business, personal, and financial life. But before execution comes preparation. Read on.

THE PROCESS FOR CHANGE STARTS WITH SETTING PRIORITIES

The first step is to sort through your list of actions and make some sense of them by setting some priorities. The goal is to come up with no more than five personal and five business actions to implement in 90-day sprints. Think of it as similar to interval training. You get your heartbeat up, rest, then do it over and over again. But what should you do first, second, and third? How do you prioritize?

GET ORGANIZED BEFORE YOU ACT

After completing the Triggering Event, you just want to get right to it. "Let's go," you think; "let's starting doing stuff." Resist the urge to take a shotgun approach. That results in disorder, frustration, and lack of accomplishment. You need to make sure you are doing the right stuff at the right time in the right order. And you want to make sure your team is capable of accomplishing the action items assigned to them. If you feel like you don't understand, go back and read the chapter on Relentless Execution.

The no-huddle offense can be very effective in football, but it doesn't work very well unless the team is already very seasoned. To run a no-huddle, everyone needs to be in sync. Their roles and tasks need to be second nature. In other words, it takes a lot of practice. It's a common mistake to expect your team to just jump on board and start cranking out actions to increase value effectively, right from the beginning. That's just not realistic. They will likely struggle in the beginning. One of the mistakes you can make is to give up too early when your team struggles to balance their present-day responsibilities while taking on the additional responsibilities of Value Acceleration. Don't give up on them; they are learning a new behavior. After they have completed a few 90-day sprints, most of your team will learn, increase cohesion, and become more effective.

To be good at relentless execution, you need to be purpose-driven, really well organized, and laser focused. The entire team needs to be connected to your vision, so you need to focus on vision first. Vision inspires action, and more importantly, sustains action. When your team is down and out and frustrated, it's the vision that keeps them going.

Once you have a clear vision statement, you want to organize your improvement actions into themes. For example, "Improving Marketing" might be a theme. Or "Management and Staff Development," or "Documentation." Use the Business Planning Pyramid as a guide to organizing your themes. Once you have themes, you need to organize projects that relate to your themes. From projects come tasks. Tasks create milestones. Milestones produce deliverables.

Vision should be at three years out. Themes are annual. Projects or actions are scoped to 90 days. Tasks are scoped to less than 90 days. Milestones are set in no more than 30-day increments.

Before we go forward, let's define what I mean by deliverables, milestones, tasks, projects, and themes. You should already understand vision (purpose). If not, go back and read the chapter on Relentless Execution. Let's start at the bottom and work our way up the ladder.

What is a "deliverable?" Deliverables represent the accomplishment of an action. A deliverable can be a report, meeting, workshop, or event that represents the conclusion of an assignment, step, stage, task, or action. Every action should produce a specific deliverable or outcome. This deliverable needs to be spelled out in detail. Ask yourself: When this action is completed, what specifically will be produced or delivered to represent the completion of the action?

It is important that the deliverable leads you to the next logical action. As such, the deliverable should recommend the next stage, step, or action that you should take and the resources needed, and it should tee up your next action. For example, Deliverable #1 in Gate One of Value Acceleration is the Triggering Event. It was composed of a Personal, Financial, and Business Assessment and a Business Valuation. And this deliverable led you to the next logical action, which is to develop a prioritized business and personal action plan. The second deliverable in Gate One is the actual business and personal prioritized action plan itself.

In Gate Two | Prepare, your deliverables will include the output from your personal, financial, and business actions. Other deliverables in Gate Two include formalization of your written Master Plan and proof (documentation) or validation of the way you scored yourself in the personal, financial, and business assessment. For example, you may have scored yourself high in marketing. The deliverable is to actually provide the detailed written marketing plan, proving that it is above average. The written marketing plan is the deliverable.

In Gate Three | Decide, your deliverable may be a workshop where you evaluated the pros and cons of all your exit options, or a workshop where you decided to keep or sell.

Milestones represent interim deliverables or steps which indicate whether or not you are on track to produce the final deliverable for the action. These milestones are important because they help you to look through the front windshield and project if the outcome of the action is likely. A milestone moves you toward passing go.

Tasks are the detailed steps that need to be completed to achieve the milestone within the specified timeframe. If these tasks are not completed, it is unlikely the milestone will be met.

Tasks are consolidated into projects. These will be the three to five prioritized actions you will establish to be completed over the next 90 days.

Finally, projects can be grouped into themes. For example, your first deliverable may have identified that your marketing is weak. To improve your marketing capability, specific actions need to be completed. You will sort through these actions and select the ones you want to pursue over the next 90 days. Once you choose your actions, you will establish tasks that need to be completed to produce a milestone. Achieving the milestones will lead you to producing the final deliverable, which represents accomplishment of the action.

Your first 90-day improvement cycle will likely be entirely dedicated to organizing and creating your action plans. After completing the Triggering Event, this will be your next major deliverable. To do it right, you will need to complete 14 workshops: seven personal and seven business. Completing the each of the workshops represents a milestone. To complete the workshops, there are tasks that need to be done to prepare, conduct, and deliver each workshop. Your theme is getting organized to execute actions. In all likelihood, this development education will consume the entire first 90-day improvement cycle. Coming out of these workshops, however, you and your teams will be extremely well-organized and laser focused: two keys to successful execution.

SETTING PRIORITIES

When organizing your actions, you want to first separate strategic from non-strategic actions. You want to defer strategic actions until after you get some experience with the system and after you have considered the "Keep or Sell" decision (addressed in Gate Three | Decide). Strategic actions require that you invest significant time and money. They take several years to implement and show a return on investment.

Your first set of priorities should be targeted at protecting what you already have through de-risking. By simply removing risk from your personal situation, your personal finances, and your business, you increase value. Remember, any risk decreases value. De-risking activities are usually fairly easy to implement. These are things like planning for unplanned events, contingency planning, completing an enterprise risk assessment, evaluating your insurance requirements, and addressing dependencies and backups.

Here is an example of what I mean. After completing the Triggering Event for a client, I learned that two of three partners did not have a financial planner. So when setting priorities, all I asked them to do in the first 90 days was to interview several financial planners and pick one. That was certainly something that could be completed in three months. And how could we move forward without financial plans for all the partners? We couldn't. I didn't ask them to complete a financial plan. That would have been too aggressive. I suggested they do that in the *next* 90 days.

It is important to keep promises, so try to keep the scope of your actions to small, incremental 90-day sprints. It's better to exceed the goal than miss it, especially in the beginning when you are building momentum.

These three owners also had a customer concentration issue. In many cases, this is a deal killer because of the risk it implies. About 30 days after setting their 90-day personal and business actions, I hosted the End of Month Accountability Team Workshop. That day, they told me they were going to hire a marketing person. I asked why were they doing that. It was not included in our 90-day action plan. Further, I asked why they would do that knowing they were planning to sell the business in the near term. They responded by explaining that I had stated in the Triggering Event management conclusions that customer concentration was an issue.

Rather than sticking to the plan, they decided they needed a marketing person to begin the process of diversifying their customer base right away. I explained that hiring a marketing person to diversify the customer base was a "strategic" initiative. It could take years for that investment to pay off.

Rather, in our Business Actions Workshop, we decided our most immediate priority should be to focus on locking in contracts with their current customers (an act of de-risking). I also suggested that developing a written diversification strategy might be something to take on in the next 90-day period (again, another de-risking action). That strategy might include hiring a marketing person, but it would depend on how long they decided to keep the business and continue growing it. If they decided to exit rather than keep it, simply having a strategy that they could explain to the potential buyer might be enough to de-risk the situation. And locking in customer contracts and developing a longer-term written customer diversification strategy were two actions that could certainly be completed in the first two 90-day implementation cycles.

Of course, a diversified customer base would add value, but so would a written strategy of how they thought it could be done and solid written transferable contracts with existing customers. These two approachable actions would add value, too, since they would partially de-risk the customer concentration issue. Do you see the difference?

After de-risking, your next priority is to evaluate your business model and build an integrated business strategy using the Business Planning Pyramid (see Chapter 8: Relentless Execution).

You will have already assessed your strengths and weaknesses in each of these areas in the Triggering Event. Next, understanding your personal and business goals, you should look at your current personal and business models and determine if they make sense given where you want to go; given your vision.

I have seen too many businesses that grow and then fall. The reason is they don't have a scalable architecture and/or the competencies needed to grow. The sales come in and the organization collapses because they are not prepared to absorb the change.

Exhibit BB: Setting Priorities

Time / effort / $ invested

Working on business efficiency, which is your third priority, also generates cash that can be used to fund longer-term initiatives. Business efficiency doesn't just include improving processes. It also includes improving your talent, improving customer delivery, improving your social operating system, installing technology, and getting your people trained.

Once you have de-risked, updated your model, and improved efficiency, you are now ready for growth, the fourth priority. Growth initiatives are typically strategic. Some of your efficiency actions are strategic as well. You don't want to take these on until you have had some experience in successful change and have internalized the Value Acceleration Methodology approach. My recommendation is that you defer efficiency and growth strategic initiatives until you have completed at least two 90-day sprints successfully. This means you are probably 9 to 12 months into the Methodology before you start looking at such initiatives.

Recall the Wow Curve discussion? It's at this time your teams are likely to be really stressed, so be reasonable in setting expectations in the beginning. You can be more aggressive once they have had successful experiences with Value Acceleration. I bet you are probably thinking, "Wow…I have to go nine to 12 months before I start growing?" Quite simply, yes.

You and your team will be so much more intelligent about your organization, your people, and your strengths and weaknesses, that you will be in a much better frame of mind to make the right strategic decisions, with a much greater probability of actually implementing them. Nine months into the Methodology, the de-risking and efficiency actions you implemented in the first few 90-day cycles will be producing increases in value. Think about it. If you hold true to the system, you will have re-established your vision, organized, trained, aligned, and focused your teams in the first three months. Then, if you execute well, you will have already implemented 10 personal and 10 business actions to grow your value and income. That alone is pretty significant, especially if your organization has not produced expected results in the past.

The final priority is culture. You may ask why culture comes last. Shouldn't developing a winning culture be first on your list? You don't build a culture; you discover it. Changing a culture is a long-term outcome, frankly. It can take years to develop strong social capital. As your organization improves and internalizes Value Acceleration, your culture will form. You can't force culture. You cannot command that "it shall be." It needs to come from success, winning, team play, and rewards.

The fact remains that not everyone on your team today will survive the change. You have probably already thought of specific players on your team who will hinder you. And it's true, a few will resist (expect about 10%), and you will need to make a change. As one of my first mentors used to say, "People *change* or *people* change."

On the other hand, some average performers today will begin to shine.

They will begin to stand out. And your "A" players (your top 20%) will flourish. The only way to find out is to test them, and provide them with tools, education, opportunity, and support. From there, you'll see who flies and who doesn't.

You want to see your team excel. And chances are, you are willing to give them training and invest in them to help them excel. But the fact is, as the company grows, not all of them will be able to grow with it. You may need to bring in new skills and new people to shore up your present team's weaknesses.

WORKSHOPS...NOT MEETINGS

Workshops are not meetings. What's the difference? The purpose of a workshop is to produce a deliverable, not just to talk within a specified amount of time. I like my workshops to last no more than two to three hours. After three hours, the energy level tends to fall and everyone gets less productive. They start thinking of everything else on their plate, getting fidgety, and losing attention.

The goal is to make sure everyone participates. You need to encourage this. I like to use a flipchart in my workshops. We write all kinds of notes on the flipcharts and hang them up around the room. Something as simple as asking someone to hang up a sheet on a wall can get them to open up and feel like they are participating. Moreover, hanging up the sheets gives everyone a visual and a sense that we are accomplishing something. And when everyone participates, it encourages buy-in. I don't believe you can force this. It has to come through the process of robust debate, robust and positive conflict, and a genuine interest in and respect for each other's points of view.

In the beginning, make sure everyone knows why they are there and what you collectively plan to accomplish or produce. Provide an example if you have one. Always start out with a little education. This is usually new to everyone there, so don't expect them to understand right away. Teach first, then get into it. It may be wise to have a preliminary workshop where you teach the concept. Give out some homework and then schedule another workshop where you will get into developing your deliverable.

It's through a series of workshops that you establish priorities, align your team, establish metrics, and a rhythm to begin Value Acceleration. I have my preferences, but as the owner, you have options on how to proceed. I don't believe there is one way to do this; I think it depends on you, your team, and the current state of your business. The best way to view Value Acceleration is as a framework or a platform to launch your value growth initiatives.

CONCURRENT BUSINESS AND PERSONAL PATHS

As I explain the types of workshops you can use to develop and implement your action plans, keep in mind you are executing on two concurrent paths: personal and business.

What about "financial," you ask? For a few practical reasons, I group financial and personal into one path, with business as the other. My first reason is that personal planning and financial planning are very tightly integrated, and both are very personal. Although there is some overlap, they tend to involve a different set of stakeholders than those involved in the business. And as financial and personal are *so personal,* you will naturally want to limit who you invite into that inner circle. Your business circle will be much larger.

Second, and also from a practical standpoint, you will prioritize no more than five personal/financial and five business actions to be completed every 90 days. That's potentially 10 actions every 90 days, on top of running your life and your business. Over the course of a year, that is 40 major actions: 20 personal/financial and 20 business. That's quite a bit of work. I believe that setting five personal, five financial, and five business actions (resulting in 15 actions over 90 days) is just not realistic. Don't get me wrong, I would love to see you accomplish 60 actions in a year with 67% of them focused on personal versus business. I just don't think you will do it.

PERSONAL AND BUSINESS ENVISIONING WORKSHOPS

Post-Triggering Event, you should immediately complete two workshops: a Personal Envisioning Workshop and a Business Envisioning Workshop. Again, I recommend you use an experienced CEPA to facilitate. Invite key members of your core team to participate, which might mean including your spouse, children, and partner(s). You generally will not include your management and other advisors at this point, primarily because these first two workshops are highly personal. They require you to dig deep to grasp and articulate your life and business long-term goals and to explore the reasons you feel strongly about them one way or another. For now, you are simply capturing your vision so that you can express it to the rest of the team in the next set of workshops.

Prior to the Envisioning Workshops:
- Revisit your attractiveness, readiness, and business valuation
- Group your actions into themes (i.e. customer, marketing, operations, finance)
- Think about where you see yourself and your business in 10 years
- Document four to five opportunities to exceed your plan and four to five risks which threaten achieving your 10-year personal vision and 10-year business vision

- Write down your core values, personal and business
- Share an example of where you have demonstrated your commitment to your core values
- Write down your mission and core purpose, both personal and business. Use the Brand Statement form available at my website.
- Why do you believe in this mission? Why do you think you can achieve it? Do you have any proof that you can achieve it?
- Why are you passionate about this mission? Explore your centers. (i.e. family, money, self...), thinking out 10 years
- Set a few three- to five-year quantitative targets. For personal and financial, these might be net worth, annual income, needs vs. wants, retirement, relocation, etc. For business, they might be business value, sales, GM, EBITDA, growth percent, markets, headcount, revenue per employee, etc...
- Write down the names of your personal and business core teams and make a list of extended/secondary team members for each. You will invite the core team (inner circle) to your next set of workshops

Consider using Verne Harnish's **Strategic Framework** as a tool to start documenting your answers. There is no need to reinvent the wheel here. Verne's system is proven. I have successfully used it in my own business ventures, and with many clients. His Strategic Framework allows you to commit your entire strategy to one piece of paper. Actually, for you, it will be two pieces of paper because you will fill one out for business and one for personal. Strategic Framework was intended to be used a business planning tool, but you can use it as personal planning tool as well. Just approach running your life like you run your business. Completing a SWOT analysis, setting core values, stating your mission or core purpose, and setting three- to five-year targets is necessary for both business and personal planning.

This exercise will enable you to eventually connect your vision to your 90-Day prioritized actions, which are called Big Rocks. In the next set of workshops, you will focus on setting 1-year and 90-day Big Rocks. You will assign responsibilities, consider options, and determine resource requirements, cost/benefits, and milestones for each 90-Day Big Rock. And that action plan will be recalibrated every 90 days.

SIX WEEKS TO BETTER BUSINESS WORKSHOPS

The outcome of the next 12 workshops will be a list of no more than five personal and five business actions you will complete in the next 90 days to start protecting and building value. These 90-day actions will be connected to your one-year goals, which will be organized around developing your three- to five-year capabilities and your three- to five-year vision. They will reflect your core values and your business and personal brand promise, and represent actions you need to take to achieve your short- and long-term targets.

In reality, I know you have many more than 10 actions you need to complete in the next 90 days. But you need to define the five personal and five business items that are the most important. This is where trade-offs are considered and choices regarding your priorities need to be hashed out with your core team. This is why it is so important to involve others in setting these priorities. It is not mandatory that you set five actions each for personal and business. You can decide on something less than that. For example, if you feel that a particular action in the next 90 days is so important that you want nothing else to distract the team from that one action, then choose only one. By selecting only one, you will clearly emphasize how important it is. In some cases, your business may already be growing and you simply don't have the time right now to focus on 10 improvement actions. These challenges are the reality of ownership.

The point is you need to prioritize well and commit to completing these actions. What you don't want is for 90 days to pass and to hear, "Well, I didn't get to that because I was working on something that was not on the 'top five' list." That's a no-no, and it indicates that you didn't pick the right "top five" or that you were just not committed enough.

This will be a truly enlightening process for you. Sometimes you find you get reinvigorated about the business and your life and decide you don't want to leave the business at all, even if that's not what you thought when you started this process. I have seen owners reengage like they did when they were first starting out. In other cases, I've seen owners who realized through the process that they were not committed enough to follow through. It helps them to recognize and discuss their lack of passion for the business at this stage of their life, ultimately deciding to expedite their exit. I was working with a client several years ago and this is just what happened.

> I was referred in by the clients' CPA because they had expressed to him that they wanted to sell. They were burned out. We went through the Triggering Event and determined they were salable but, of course, not at the price they were hoping. I pointed out, however, that there were lots of opportunities to improve the business. It would take some time and work, but if they worked on these opportunities, we could drive up the price and value in the marketplace. We completed the personal and business workshops and came up with five personal and five business actions that could be completed in the next 90 days. I suggested we defer the decision to go to market for 90 days; instead, we would first try to implement some de-risking improvement actions. It's the work we would have to do anyway to get the business ready for market, so the time would be well spent either way.

> "Let's just save the conversation about exit until after we have completed the first 90-day sprint," I suggested.

Well, as we went through the workshops, one of the two partners got very excited. I could tell she didn't really want to exit. In reality, she was only considering exiting because she was frustrated with her partner, who she felt was not passionate about the business anymore, and in turn, was not carrying his end of the load. She saw the opportunity to implement these changes as a way to possibly get her partner reengaged. One priority was assigned to the management team and the other four to her and her partner, as the owners.

As we went through the 90-day cycle, the management team did well, hitting all their milestones. But the two owners missed all of their milestones, including the partner who said she didn't want to exit!

At the Quarterly Renewal Workshop, only one of the five priorities was complete. Guess which one. Of course, it was the one assigned to the management team. In fact, the management team had exceeded their goal. Zero of the four assigned to the owners were complete. It was a bit embarrassing for the owners, so I took them aside for a private meeting.

"What's going on?" I asked.

They started to give me all kinds of excuses. This came up and that came up. All excuses.

"What's really going on?" I asked. "We agreed, didn't we, that these four things were a priority. Did we pick the wrong things?"

"No," said the owners, "these were the right things."

"Then why didn't you get them done?" I asked. "I know that when you view something as important, you get it done. If we picked the right things and if you are really committed, you would have gotten them done. No? You guys are really talented and you have built a great business. You know how to get things done if you really want to. So why did you miss on these?"

"We realized we are both burned out. We just don't want to do this anymore," the owners said.

"We've lost our passion for it. We want to get on with our lives and do something else," said the owner who previously told me she did not want to exit (the one who was initially high on the Wow Curve), "We're not committed anymore. We just want out."

"Okay, fair enough," I said. "Let's focus our next 90 days on the activities to get into something new."

Remember early on, when I said one of the big deliverables of the Triggering Event process is clarity? This exercise helped these owners figure out what they really wanted—or, more accurately, what they didn't want anymore. The decision to leave the business was now clear. We moved in the direction of exiting the business with rigor and six months later, sold it. The owners didn't get what they wanted in terms of price. But they got something much more than that: peace of mind and a new life.

Below is a description of each of the workshops, which are inspired by Verne Harnish's "Rockefeller Habits." Your core teams, including your key people, personal and business, should participate in the workshops, though the personal and business workshops will likely involve different people. You will complete all six workshops for business and for personal, totaling 12 workshops over 90 days. The workshops should be timed and last no more than three hours. If you are using a facilitator, which I highly recommend, the facilitator will take notes and publish the decisions and results. If you do use a facilitator, make sure you use someone who has experience, like a CEPA. This is a big investment and you want to make sure you deliver a great result.

I have noted the deliverable for each of the workshops below. I want to take a few minutes to describe a particularly important one, delivered in Workshop 4 - Alignment, called the Opportunity Assessment. Once you have determined and assigned the 90-day actions to a champion (which could be you), the champion is required to produce an Opportunity Assessment within one week of concluding Workshop 3, which is where you will determine and assign your actions. These actions become mini-projects to be completed in 90 days.

Each champion should go through the process of scoping his or her project and presenting the project back to the team. There will be one Opportunity Assessment for each action. The Opportunity Assessment defines the scope, tasks, alternative ways to approach completing the action (or project), resources required, cost/benefits, and most importantly, the milestones that need to be met to measure if the project is on time.

You will use these Opportunity Assessments at your Mid-Month 1:1 Check-In Workshops (which I will explain to you in the next chapter). I think it's a good idea for the champions to actually fill out a form when doing this because requiring them to complete the form forces them to really articulate the details behind getting their project accomplished.

Exhibit CC: Workshops | Not Meetings

Workshop 1 — Education **Deliverable:** Team Educated on the Value Acceleration Methodology	This includes overall education on the process and the expected outcomes of each workshop; the roles of each person participating; and some general education on how to manage the growth process, both personal and business. Usually, different teams are involved for personal versus business. Both should include key people in your personal life and business. Summarize the results of the personal, financial, and business assessments and valuation. Share a summary of the strengths, weaknesses, and themes. This is your first opportunity to begin teaching your teams about value.
Workshop 2 — Strategic Framework Focus on next three- to five-year vision **Deliverable:** Three- to Five-Year Goals and Priorities	You will begin this workshop by sharing with the team the output from your envisioning workshops, which includes opportunities and risks, core values, vision, and targets. This is your opportunity to inspire the team and begin the process of connecting them to your vision. After you share your vision, ask your team to comment. Write all this stuff on flipcharts and hang them up around the room. Time each section so that you can complete the workshop in no more than three hours. Your output includes: • Share/validate opportunities and risks. • Share/validate core values. • Share/validate core purpose/primary aim. • Share/discuss actions (deliverables) you have completed in the last 90 days which demonstrate your commitment to your core values. • Share/validate your 10-year goal. • Validate your three- to five-year quantifiable targets (for business: value, revenues, profit, market share; or for personal: net worth, annual income, needs vs. wants) and the two areas where you think you can dominate. • Share/validate tour brand statement. • Define three- to five-year capabilities (priorities) to dominate and reach three- to five-year targets. • Define metrics that give you feedback.

Workshop 3 — Focus is on the next year and quarter **Deliverable:** One-Year and Next Quarter Goals and Priorities	• Define upcoming one-year goals (quantified, ex: revenues, profits, net worth, personal income, etc.). • Define no more than five key initiatives (priorities) over the next year. • Define next quarter goals (quantified, ex: revenues, profits, etc.) and top five priorities. • Define a few key performance metrics (KPIs) for both one year and next quarter which measure progress and provide feedback. KPIs are key weaknesses which, if addressed, will have a significant and positive impact on the business or your personal situation. • Using priorities, KPIs, and goals establish a quarterly theme, design a scoreboard, and decide how you will celebrate your accomplishments. • Assign each priority to a champion. • Assign the work to be prepared for the next workshop (Opportunity Assessment).
Workshop 4 — Alignment **Deliverable:** Opportunity Assessment	This workshop is with those who were assigned a quarterly priority. Each champion will describe their action/project using the Opportunity Assessment format. Start the workshop by confirming the top five priorities. Each champion takes a turn and presents the following for their action item: • Description of action, history, and why it is important. What problem are we trying to solve or what opportunity are we trying to jump on? • Alternatives considered • Suggested action from the alternatives considered • High level cost/benefit • Timeline and team structure • Three to five milestones • Description of the deliverable • Define and commit resource requirements • Define who is accountable for each task on the plan • Name an accountability buddy

Workshop 5 — Metrics and Feedback System **Deliverable:** Individual and Company Dashboards	In this workshop, you will develop a handful of key performance metrics that will provide weekly, monthly, and quarterly feedback. You continue to align the team to these metrics and develop a company dashboard. • Confirm the quarterly theme. • Define success factors. • Define key metrics. • Design (create) dashboards: personal and company. • Agree on how to make dashboards visible.
Workshop 6 — Rhythm **Deliverable:** Meeting and Workshop Rhythm	In this final workshop, establish the meeting and workshop rhythm to be used by the personal and business core teams. • Mid-Month 1:1 Check-In Workshop • Monthly Accountability Workshop • Quarterly Renewal Workshop • Set Quarterly Renewal Workshop Dates • Assign ownership of the calendar

After concluding these workshops, you and your teams will be ready to execute. You will have sorted through all the value factors that are holding your value down and grouped them into themes. From this list of "stuff," you will produce a prioritized list of no more than five business and five personal actions to complete over the next 90 days. These actions will be connected to your one-year and three-year goals, your vision, and your core values and purpose.

Each action will be assigned to a champion. This champion will have analyzed their project and scoped it to a 90-day deliverable in the form of the Opportunity Assessment (see Workshop 4), which has established three to five milestones to demonstrate it is on track. You and the champion will review progress toward these milestones twice a month. Your team will have established a set of metrics, which both predict you are on track and measure results. Finally, you will have established a communication protocol, with future workshops already scheduled on everyone's calendar.

STEPPING THROUGH GATE ONE

The assessment conducted in the Triggering Event and the completion of these workshops to create prioritized action plans represent the deliverables for Gate One | Discover in the Value Acceleration Methodology. Even with this discovery in hand, though, you still have not delivered any change. Everything to this point has been focused around education, planning, and organization. You are organized and now you need to execute. Without relentless execution, all of your plans are pointless.

CHAPTER ELEVEN

GATE TWO | PREPARE: Delivering Action Plans

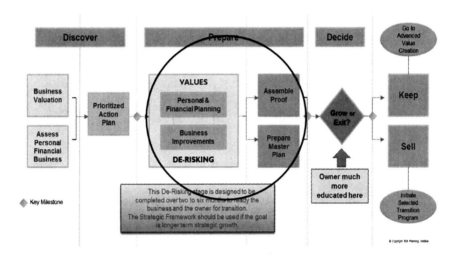

Exhibit S: The Value Acceleration Methodology

At this point, you have established and shared your vision. You have put a fantastic plan together and created focus by including your core team in the process of debating and selecting priorities. You assigned these priorities to yourself or to a champion on your team. You have educated your team on the Value Acceleration approach and reinforced the importance of achieving their assigned action items. They also now understand the impact of their actions on the value of the business.

The Prepare Gate is about execution. That is why I think it is the most important step in your journey. I can't emphasize enough how important it is to have solid execution and delivery rhythm. It is only through delivery that you demonstrate your commitment to achieving a better life and a better business. As Wallace D. Wattles wrote, in *The Science of Getting Rich*, "Use your mind to form a mental image of what you want, and hold that vision with faith and purpose; and use your will to keep your mind working in the Right Way." Further, Wattles writes, "...you must not rely upon thought alone, paying no attention to personal action. That is the rock upon which many otherwise scientific metaphysical thinkers meet shipwreck."

Just Do It
Distant People

I'll tell you we as a people
Have something special
A blessing inside
Always in search of that one thing
To bring a better way

We all fall down sometimes
But we gotta get up
Take a step, go out
And just do it

Delivering action is about focus, reinforcement, and accountability. One of the keys is moderation; do not overload yourself or your team. Take big projects and break them down into 90-day incremental deliverables. Remember to think in terms of sprints and interval training.

Wattle writes, "Hold the vision of yourself in the right business, with the purpose to get into it, and the faith that you will get into it, and are getting into it; but *act* in your present business."

You can only act in the present—not the past and not the future. Remember what was said about exit planning and changing your paradigm in the beginning of this book? You build a better exit by focusing your action on *now*. That *now* is your five personal and five business actions that you need to complete in the next 90 days. Surely you can hold your attention for 90 days. After 90 days, you will recalibrate, reset, recommit, and proceed into another 90 days. But for now, focus on what you can do in the next 90 days.

Imagine if you were able to accomplish five personal and five business improvement actions every quarter for a year. You would accomplish 40 improvements in a year, an incredible accomplishment by most standards.

The key is to focus on the right things and get the right things done. Every action can be broken down into its incremental tasks and milestones. Doing those things, task by task, accomplishment by accomplishment, will lead to achieving your ultimate goal. Those are the critical success factors, the milestones to achieving your vision and driving value.

Your team will need help and you will need to reinforce the process. You can't delegate ownership of Value Acceleration. You need to own it. Remember that change is really difficult, and risky. Some of your team will have the old "this too shall pass" attitude. Your perseverance and the direct commitment of your time will send a reinforcing message to the entire team. That will be more important than ever in the beginning as you start the process of execution.

Think of the Prepare Gate as a series of 90-day sprints toward accomplishing 10 prioritized actions. You will move on the two concurrent paths, personal and business, and recalibrate every 90 days. If you have completed the workshops in Gate One properly, these 90-day actions will be the means to accomplish your one-year goals, which lead to accomplishing your three- to five-year goals. Your three- to five-year goals will be focused around creating the competencies you need to build to achieve your targets, which are a reflection of your vision.

To help you with implementation, I recommend a series of workshops I designed to manage your time efficiently and reinforce the action necessary to accomplish your priorities. You use three types of workshops in the Prepare Gate.

MID-MONTH 1:1 CHECK-IN WORKSHOP

Each month hold a Mid-Month 1:1 Check-In Workshop. These are individual sessions with your project champions. They should last no more than two to three hours each.

Pull the Opportunity Assessments created in Gate One for each action. Check to see how well your champions are making progress toward their deliverable and milestones due at the end of the month. Have they run into hurdles that you can help remove? Do they need some education? Maybe they need some time with you to brainstorm their next tasks. You may need to share an example again or help them work through the design of their solution.

Spend an at least an hour or two with them, helping them succeed and prepare for the End of Month Accountability Team Workshop, where they will need to present a status report to the entire team. You can accomplish this with something as simple as a phone call. I prefer face-to-face. With the workshop, there is no agenda per se, but there should be a planned outcome. Let your champion decide what he or she wants to accomplish with you. But make sure at the beginning it is clear what your deliverable is for the workshop. Remember, workshops not meetings.

The main purpose of the Mid-Month 1:1 Check-In Workshop is to provide guidance, if needed, to help your champion prepare to deliver a project status at the End of Month Accountability Team Workshop. This usually involves reviewing one of the milestones they were scheduled to hit during the previous month.

If you check in and your champion indicates everything is good to go, it may not even be necessary to continue with the workshop. Workshops that don't have a purpose are meetings. You don't want a meeting. If you are going to spend time together, make sure there is something that will be accomplished. But beware...your champions may be saying that it is not necessary to have the workshop because they want you to *think* everything is okay.

With the Opportunity Assessment in front of you, ask them some specific questions: Does the description of the action still make sense? Have you received all the resources you said you needed? Does the cost/benefit analysis still seem realistic? Are you still on track to hit all your milestones? Answers to these specific questions will allow you to assess whether things are really on track or not. If you are the champion, use this time to assess your own progress or meet with your accountability buddy.

I inserted this Mid-Month 1:1 Check-In Workshop into the 90-day improvement cycle because it's very likely many of your champions will struggle, especially in the beginning, with execution. They will show up for the End of Month Accountability Team Workshop with missed milestones, excuses, and poor presentations. It becomes frustrating for you and the others on the team who made the effort to accomplish their milestones and prepare properly. The check-in gives you an opportunity to meet with your champion in advance, one-on-one before the team status deadline, to make sure he or she is on track and to reinforce the commitment to delivery—both yours and theirs. This avoids awkward and embarrassing situations at the monthly accountability workshops, which need to be crisp and positive to be effective.

Over time, your team will get better with all of these processes after completing a few cycles of the Value Acceleration Methodology and as the culture starts to evolve.

Don't forget about your personal actions. You will facilitate these same Mid-Month 1:1 Check-In Workshops with your personal team, too. Now, you might be thinking, "Wow, this is a lot of time I need to spend. Can I do this as a team workshop instead of one-on-one with each team member?"

You can, but I would not recommend it. The "1:1" is that special time that you and your champion get to spend to really zero in on their action item. It is an opportunity to teach, encourage, and motivate. It gives your champion time to pick your brain and have your full attention. To ensure your time is well spent, reinforce adherence to the system. If someone calls for a meeting, ask them if it can wait until the Mid-Month 1:1 Check-In Workshop, where you will have already reserved the time and they will have your full attention. Doing this develops discipline. It also teaches them to carry on without you and to make decisions without you. And that is good for their development and addresses the owner dependence issue in most middle market businesses.

If you are short on time, seriously consider bringing in a CEPA to help you. I have played this role for many owners over the years. Owners have asked me to help oversee some or even all of their action items and teams, and we split up the workload.

It just depends on how much time you want and have to spend. CEPAs can do this with mature and deeply talented management teams as well as immature, first-line managers in small businesses. That said, the more time you require from a CEPA, the more fees are involved. However, the fees are truly minor compared to the literal value being generated.

Justifying using a CEPA, or any outside advisor for that matter, really depends on your point of view. Do you view your advisors as an expense or an investment? If you don't view the advisors working with you as "investments," you should get new advisors. Advisors should be held accountable to produce, just like any other employee in the company. They need to produce more resources than they consume. If you (and they) can't see that, you probably don't have the right advisor sitting at your table.

THE END OF MONTH ACCOUNTABILITY TEAM WORKSHOP

The Mid-Month 1:1 Check-In Workshop is your time to spend one-on-one time with each champion. Every 30 days, you must hold a full team workshop, called the End of Month Accountability Team Workshop, where each champion presents the status of his or her priority to the rest of the team. If possible, I like to have them actually prepare a PowerPoint to present to the team. This forces them to really think about where they are, be professional, and articulate an accurate description of the status of their priority in a formal presentation to the rest of the team.

For my clients and employees, I provide a template for this. But you can prepare one yourself and have everyone on the team use the same format. The first time, it will take some time to design it. But thereafter, it will be a piece of cake. This also encourages ownership. No one likes to be embarrassed by coming into the workshop unprepared. It also forces team accountability. If four of your champions have prepared properly and one has not, peer pressure is exerted on the underperformer. Or perhaps the underperformer really has an issue completing the tasks associated to his or her priority, and by their lack of preparation or effort, you gain clarity that they truly need help. I have seen great teams rally in support. The emphasis of the presentations is to demonstrate champions' progress toward achieving their milestones. Are they on track? If not, why not? If so, let's recognize them and celebrate accomplishment.

THE QUARTERLY RENEWAL WORKSHOP (EVERY 90 DAYS)

Every 90 days, hold a half- to full-day Quarterly Renewal Workshop, preferably offsite. In the beginning, it might take a full day to do this. Once you have some experience with the Renewal Process, you get more efficient with it and can likely do it in a half day. Bear in mind that a side benefit of this workshop is team bonding. You might even consider combining it with a recreational or team outing as part of the process. The spirit of this workshop is accountability and renewal. Below is an example of an agenda for the Quarterly Renewal Workshop:

Exhibit DD: Sample Quarterly Offsite Agenda
The Club at Key Center

7:30 – 8:30	Kickoff, Management Team Exercise (John - Owner) (Continental breakfast)
8:30 – 9:45	Q2 Accomplishments and Disappointments • John to do overview (15 minutes) • Michelle (15 minutes) • Patty (15 minutes) • Joe (15 minutes) • Sean (15 minutes)
9:45 – 10:15	Break (30 minutes)
10:15 – 11:45	Q3 Top Five Priorities Setting (Establish)
12:00 – 1:30	Lunch (out)
1:30 – 2:45	Finish Top Five Priorities (Prioritize and Assign)
2:45 – 3:00	Break
3:00 – 3:30	Metrics/Rhythm
3:30 – 4:00	Wrap Up

ACCOMPLISHMENTS AND DISAPPOINTMENTS

The first part of the workshop will focus on the previous 90 days. Each champion presents their deliverable from the previous 90 days to the rest of the team. There is usually some dialogue back and forth about it. Next, sum up the quarter by doing a simple exercise of accomplishments and disappointments. Write them on a flipchart and hang them up on the wall.

ESTABLISH PRIORITIES

Take a break. After the break, look at your vision, three- to five-year competency goals, brand statement, and metrics. Given what has happened in the last 90 days, should anything be reexamined or changed? Are there any new strengths, weaknesses, threats, or opportunities? If so, write them on the flipchart and hang them up. We will consider these when we set our next 90-day priorities. Revisit your annual initiatives, targets, and metrics. Does anything here need to change? If so, write it on the flipchart.

Next, begin the debate on the priorities for next 90 days. It is helpful to have the notes from the previous quarterly workshop in front of you. For advance prep, have each person write down what they think should be the top three priorities in the next 90 days before coming to the workshop. Then have each person write their ideas on the flipchart. Hang them up. Stay in green light mode—focus on idea generation. Don't start debating the priorities yet or discussing why something can't be done. For now, stay in green light and write down all the ideas.

PRIORITIZE AND ASSIGN PRIORITIES

Take a break. After the break, group the initiatives, keeping in mind your themes from the personal, financial, and business assessments. Now move into yellow and red light, debating back and forth which items should be established as the Top Five. Put a time limit on the discussion. Reach consensus. Vote if you have to, by having each person write a 1, 2, and 3 on sticky pad sheets, then posting them on the actions they think should be 1, 2, or 3. Then stand back and choose. If the group can't come to a consensus, you as the owner must decide.

As with many of these things, the process is more important than the actual choice. Don't dwell on whether it should be this or that. Pick one and move on. The idea that we are actually having this kind of discussion and making these kinds of choices is the most important benefit. You are only committing for 90 days, so it's not likely to be the end of the world if you choose one or two of these actions incorrectly.

Once decided, ask, "Who wants to be the champion for each of these actions?" You will usually get some volunteers. If you are comfortable with the volunteer, approve it. If not, you should discuss it with the team. Sometimes people will volunteer for things they simply don't have time to do or are not qualified to do. Deal with the brutal facts and make the call. False kindness is not useful here.

Assign a scribe to the workshop; bring an assistant; or, if your workshop is facilitated by a CEPA, have them take notes, distribute the notes to everyone who attended, and include a list of follow-up items. If you get stuck on something, put it on a side board as something that needs to be addressed after the workshop. Assign each item to a person who is responsible for following up.

METRICS/RHYTHM

Take a break. Before you leave, spend 30 to 60 minutes revisiting your metrics and rhythm. How is your rhythm? Are communications appropriate and effective? If not, write that down. Do the metrics we track need to be changed? What's our next quarter theme? Write it all down.

Now, go back and use the process of creating Opportunity Assessments in Gate One. Within one week of the Quarterly Renewal Workshop, hold a follow-up workshop where the champions present their Opportunity Assessments. You should discuss their thought process for the analysis and justification for the prioritized action, the resources required, the deliverable, and the milestones as a team. Often, a manager may be the champion of one action and an extended team member on another. Discuss and work out resource constraints. Also, follow up on any changes to your metrics and company rhythm as a result of your new Top Five and decide on your quarterly theme.

Remember, you don't have to pick five. It can be less. If there is a really critical project or resource limitation, you can pick less than five actions to accomplish. Find your team's rhythm. Identify which one of the five is the most important and get consensus from the team.

You will perform a similar Quarterly Renewal Workshop with your personal team, reviewing your personal accomplishments and disappointments. Then select five personal actions for the next 90 days just like you did with your business team. This time, your personal team might include your spouse, your children, and other family members who may not be active in the business. This gives them a chance to participate. If you have partners in the business, I suggest you do this together. It would also benefit you to include your personal financial planner, and perhaps your legal counsel. If you have a life coach, they would be included. The more people from your inner circle, the better, as you will likely be assigning them one of the priorities.

UPDATE YOUR SCORECARD

Once you have completed at least two 90-day cycles, go back and rescore yourself using the personal, financial, and business assessment process we completed in Gate One. Place the value of the business in the range of value that you started with as a baseline. You will see the quantitative benefits happening right before your eyes. By rescoring and relating this to your new, higher place in the range of value, you will witness a quantitative measurement of Value Acceleration.

CHAPTER TWELVE

GATE THREE | DECIDE: Grow or Exit?

Exhibit S: The Value Acceleration Methodology

The Decide Gate coincides with the Harvest Stage of Value Maturity. Scoring well on the Value Maturity Index in this stage means you have thoroughly considered the pros and cons of each of the exit options. Moreover, you have thoroughly considered the risks and commitments necessary to strategically accelerate growth in value. Take your time in this Gate. When I use the words "Sell" or "Exit," understand that I use them in the context of any inside or outside exit choice.

You should visit this decision, Grow or Exit, every 90 days! This brings the keep or sell choice into the present. In either case, you will cycle back through the Creating Action Plans step in Gate One and set priorities based on your decision. If you choose the Sell path, you will prioritize actions that focus more on getting you prepared to sell. If you choose the Keep path, you will give growth actions higher priority.

What's the difference? This is a major decision for you, so take it seriously. If you decide to keep

---
Deal
Grateful Dead

Since it cost a lot to win
And even more to lose
You and me bound to spend some time
Wondering what to choose

Goes to show you don't ever know
Watch each card you play
And play it slow
Wait until that deal come round
Don't you let that deal go down

---

growing, you will invest in that path, which could mean taking on more debt, more people, and more complexity, which are all strategic in nature. You need to be personally committed and willing to assume the risks associated with growth. If you choose to sell, you will likely emphasize the opposite, focusing on less debt, less risk, and preserving earnings. The choice is a strategic one, as it is a multi-year commitment either way and there is a cost for shifting back and forth. For example, if you make a strategic investment to grow and then decide to sell before it has a chance to pay off, you may not accomplish the full return you expected from the investment. If you decide to sell now, you will likely be foregoing many opportunities for growth and value enhancement.

This is why I recommend you kick this can down the road and don't consider the choice seriously until after you have completed at least two 90-day sprints, focusing on de-risking in the Prepare Gate. You never know if tragedy will strike, and at least 50% of the time, it does strike (recall the Five D's?). Furthermore, if you do complete at least a few 90-day cycles, you will be much wiser, more in touch with personal goals, personal energy, and risk sensitivity, and you will be in a much better place to choose what you want to focus on over the next several years.

I have worked with owners who thought they wanted to sell but realized, after completing a couple cycles of Value Acceleration, that they were reinvigorated and wanted to make a run at Advanced Value Acceleration (AVA). On the other hand, I have worked with owners who thought they wanted to sell to a third party, but after researching their options, determined that a sale to management or employees fit better with their personal and financial goals and objectives.

> One of my past clients scored 61% (slightly above the midpoint) on his Attractiveness Assessment and 82% (well into the best-in-class premium level) on his Readiness Assessment. This meant the business was average from an attractiveness standpoint, yet the owner and the business were very prepared to transition. This is unusual. In most cases, the attractiveness score is higher than the readiness score. He told me that he was looking at a five-year horizon (the magic five years) to exit his business. His market was flat.
>
> I asked him, "Why five years?"
>
> He said he was only 55 and not ready personally to exit now; given five more years, he still had time to drive value into the business. He had completed actions to protect value and prepare for the day he would exit. This was reflected in his high readiness score.
>
> *Good thinking*, I thought.

He was giving himself time to build value. However, the market he was in was flat with no prospects for it growing anytime soon.

So I asked him, "Where's the growth going to come from? Your market is flat and not growing."

He thought for a moment and answered, "We haven't figured that out yet."

"Well," I said, "you scored really high on your Readiness Assessment. One of the highest we have ever had. You were either not being honest or you really are very prepared to exit. But I realize you are still very engaged in the business. Your attractiveness score showed us that the business is slightly above average, with some room for improvement. One of your strengths is your really strong management team and long-term tenured employees. Your systems, processing, and customer relationships are also above average and you have a strong leader in marketing. And you said you are not in a hurry and still engaged."

"Yeah...so what is your question?"

"WHY AREN'T YOU BUYING?!"

"What do you mean?" he asked, bewildered.

"Well, if you're not in a hurry and the market is flat, the only way to grow is to acquire another business in your market, consolidate, and take market share. It certainly seems that given your scores, your reputation in the market, and your size, there would be synergies that could be created if you acquired players in your industry that are not as strong as you and integrate them into a highly efficient model. Perhaps you should consider talking to a private equity company. You are approaching $50 million in sales and have a pretty strong forecasted EBITDA. Partnering with a private equity company would not only bring in the capital you need to do a roll-up, but expertise to accomplish it. Plus, you could take some chips off the table so you weren't risking all the value you have built into the business."

"Hmmm, that's something."

"Have you ever spoken to any private equity firms?" I asked.

"Well, no," said the owner, "I was just thinking I would sell in five years."

"To whom? How do you know what the market will be like in five years?" I asked.

"Ha, I don't," said the owner. "That's why I brought you in. I expected you to know."

"Well, I have an idea, but who really knows for sure? In your opinion, how accurate have market forecasters been in the past?" I asked.

"They usually don't know s***," he laughed.

"Exactly. No one knows for sure. I know that I don't want you expecting that five years from now, the market will be as strong as it is now," I continued. "If that's your strategy, you need to be ready to sell when I tell you it's time. That could be a year from now, three years from now, or five years from now. Who really knows? We can keep an eye on it, but trying to time the market is not something I advocate. It's impossible to really know. In my entire career, I've only seen someone time the market perfectly once."

"You have a great management team and employees," I continued. "Have you considered an ESOP or management team buy-out?"

"I don't know anything about those options," he said.

"Well, you aren't in a hurry; that would give us time to do some tax and estate planning and examine the pros and cons of selling to your employees or management."

"Thinking about it now, a while ago, of my managers did express some interest in buying the company," said the owner, "and I'm sure if I asked the employees, there might be some interest."

"Okay then," I said, "why don't we take some time over the next couple of 90-day cycles and talk to a few PE firms. They won't charge you for this. I know several I have worked with that might be a good fit. I can arrange for you to meet them and discuss the PE model. I can also introduce you to a couple ESOP firms. There is a great one located nearby called the Ohio Employee Ownership Center. They are a not-for-profit and have a relationship with Kent State University. Their mission is to help owners explore this option. In fact, they have an upcoming conference. Maybe we should attend to get more educated on the subject and speak with some other companies that have successfully done an ESOP. I am sure they would be willing to introduce us to a few ESOP companies they have worked with. I could also introduce you to Enterprise Services Inc. (ESI). They are a nationally recognized

ESOP consulting and valuation firm with more than 500 clients. Scott Miller, the managing partner, is a member of EPI's faculty and a board member of EPI. I'm certain he would talk to you and provide you with some education. And I know a few attorneys who are members of the NEO Chapter of EPI. They understand the Value Acceleration Methodology and have done a number of management buyouts. While we're at it, let's also talk to some investment banking firms in town to get their perspective on the market. After all this, we may still decide selling to a strategic buyer is the best option. But you should explore all your options before you decide."

"Agreed."

EXIT/SELL—ARE YOU READY?

The first thing you want to consider when deciding to sell is whether or not you are *ready* to sell. From my experience with buy-side searches that when I call on a business, I can tell from a short conversation whether an owner is ready or not. If they are not ready, I'll suggest they contact a CEPA in their area and begin the process of getting ready, and then I move on. I might talk to 40 owners in a search and pursue only two, because the other 38 are not prepared. I often wonder if these owners realize they may have just missed their golden opportunity to sell at a premium. And I wonder if they will ever get another opportunity and what will happen to them if they don't get their act together. You never know when opportunity will knock. One day, out of the blue, you may get a call from someone like me who wants to purchase your business. Will you be ready?

During the process of preparing the questions for the EPI *State of Owner Readiness Survey,* one of the team members asked me what seemed like an obvious question, "How does an owner know if he or she is ready?" That seemed like a simple and obvious question that deserved an answer. Below is a set of 10 simple statements to help you determine what you need to accomplish to be prepared, or "ready," to sell your business. Use this simple checklist.

EXHIBIT EE: Are You Ready? | 10 Things To Determine If You Are

You are "Prepared" or "Ready" to sell your business if:

1. You have spent some time and money getting educated on the process of how to transition your business. You have discussed transitioning with your loved ones.
2. Your personal, financial, and business goals are aligned, meaning they are defined, co-dependent, and linked.
3. You have created an advisory team that includes, at minimum: an attorney, CPA, wealth or financial advisor, CEPA, spouse or partner or other family who is a "significant other" in your life. Other advisors may be included as well: personal friends, banking advisor, M&A attorney, estate planning attorney, real estate attorney, business attorney, ESOP specialist, tax specialist, insurance specialist, foundation/charity representative, key employees, investment banker or business broker, board members, family, or personal counselor.
4. You have created a contingency plan, which should include: buy-sell instructions; appropriate insurance; and basic estate planning legal documents (i.e., will, POAs, trusts). The plan should specify what should happen if, before you transition, something was to happen outside of your control that would prevent you from

operating your business or unwillingly force you to transition. You have reviewed this plan with your trusted advisors, including family members and/or partners, if applicable.

5. You have completed a strategic analysis, business valuation, and personal, financial, and business assessment(s) within the past year.
6. You have considered all of your exit options and optimum deal structure and weighed the pros and cons of each in relation to your stated goals and objectives.
7. Your transition plan is written and includes: goals and objectives; clearly defined tasks and accountabilities; definition of your transition team; definition of your transition process; a plan leader or project manager (i.e., CEPA and Value Advisor); timelines; a budget; and your role before, during, and after transition. This plan ideally has a multi-year implementation timeline.
8. You have considered and designed a post-business life-after plan. This plan is linked to, or is part of, your wealth management plan, which has been prepared by a professional financial advisor, and, if applicable, estate planning attorney, insurance specialist, tax specialist, and charitable foundation specialist.
9. You have a pre-transition value enhancement/preliminary due diligence project underway to de-risk the business, maximize its value, minimize taxes upon transition, and improve the probability of a smooth transition to the next owner, including family, partners, or employees, if applicable. Family transitions should be treated no differently than other transition options. This plan ideally has a multi-year implementation timeline.
10. You have a management succession program underway to ensure the post-transition leadership is prepared to operate the company after you exit and have secured the appropriate specialists to handle your desired transition option.

CONSEQUENCES OF NOT BEING READY

If you have not completed all of these success factors, you are not ready, and there are serious consequences to attempting to transition if you are not ready. The likelihood that you will be one of the owners in the Price Waterhouse survey who profoundly regretted the exit decision is very high. You will not maximize the value of your business at the time of exit. You are not financially prepared. And you are not personally prepared, in accordance with the Three Legs of the Stool. Many tax, estate planning, and charitable gifting strategies need several years to fully maximize your net proceeds. Net proceeds are what you keep versus what you sell for. That is the number you really want to have a handle on. Net proceeds reflect what you keep after paying taxes, professional fees, and sale expenses.

If you have not completed a personal plan for what you are going to do next and have not considered how you will fund it, it is highly likely you will be bored and miserable and a lot less rich than you think. If you don't believe me, talk to other owners who have sold without having a written plan for what they are going to do next. Many wander around for years, wondering what to do with their life. On the contrary, owners who have a written plan for what they want to do next and have taken steps to position themselves have wonderful next acts. Yes, you need to write down your plan. If your plans are not written, they are simply ideas and unlikely to be accomplished.

If you decide to sell to a third party, it is likely that your deal will not close—or in order to get it to close, the original offer will be modified lower and you will not receive the original offer price. The buyer may hold to the original price and modify the terms to lower the cash delivered at close, requiring you to accept hold-backs, earn-outs, or contingent notes so that you bear the risks. Even if you decide to transition to employees, family, partners, or management, the chances of succeeding with this transition will be very low. That can turn into real problem for you, as inside transition options do not usually include big up-front liquidity benefits. And if the business has issues going forward, which is likely if you have not prepared properly, you put getting your full payout at risk.

EXIT OPTIONS

If you decide to sell, remember that it's not like you can do this quickly (or at least you shouldn't look at trying to do this quickly). It takes serious time and financial commitment to do it right, and you don't want to rush it. At EPI, we generally recognize eight primary exit options: four inside and four outside.

Inside options are:

- Intergenerational Transfer
- Management Buyout
- Sale to Existing Partners
- Employee Stock Ownership Plan (ESOP)

Outside options are:

- Sale to Third Party
- Recapitalization
- IPO
- Orderly Liquidation

IPO is a valid exit option. But I will not spend any time on it because most businesses in the lower to middle market do not realistically have this option available to them. There are exceptions, but for the vast majority of lower and middle market businesses, IPO is not a real option.

EXIT OPTIONS ANALYSIS

Now let's explore the pros and cons of each of our options:

Intergenerational Transfer

The transfer of business stock to direct heirs, usually children. About half of business owners want to exercise this option; in reality, only about 30% actually do so.

Pros	Cons
• Business Legacy Preservation • Planned • Lower Cost • More Control • Less Disruption • High Buyer/Seller Motivation	• Family Dynamics • Illiquid Buyers/Lack Funds • Lower Sale Price • Key Employee Flight Risk • Tradition May Outstrip Good Strategy • Path of Least Resistance (but not always a path to growth or success)

Management Buyout (MBO)

Owner sells all or part of the business to the company's management team. Management uses the assets of the business to finance a significant portion of the purchase price.

Pros	Cons
• Continuity • Highly Motivated Buyers (Pent-Up Desire) • Preserves Key Human Capital / Knowledge • Planned • Can be combined with Private Equity to access additional capital and resources for growth	• Management "Sand-Bagging" • Distraction • Threat of Flight (Coercion of Owner) • Illiquid Buyers • Lower Price and Unattractive Deal Terms for Seller • Heavy Seller Financing introduces risk • Managers are Not Always Good Entrepreneurs

Sale to Existing Partners

Success is closely linked to the existence and quality of a buy-sell agreement. Not available to single-owner businesses.

Pros	Cons
• Less disruptive • Planned • Well-informed buyers • Controlled process--if Buy-Sell Agreement in place and funded • Lower cost	• Lower sales price • Potential discord • Competency gaps? • Buy-Sell may restrict selling options • Realization of proceeds from sale is often slower (and smaller)

Employee Stock Ownership Plan (ESOP)

Company uses borrowed funds to acquire shares from the owner and contributes the shares to a trust on behalf of the employees.

Pros	Cons
• Business stays in the "extended family" • Shares purchased with pre-tax dollars by the ESOP • Taxable gain on the shares sold to the ESOP by the owner may sometimes be deferred • ESOP is an employee benefit • May cause employees to think and act like owners	• Complicated and expensive • Requires securities registration exemption • Company compelled to buy back shares from departing employees • Generally suitable only for gradual exit over time

Sale to Third Party

Owner sells the business to a strategic buyer, financial buyer, or private equity group through a negotiated sale, controlled auction, or unsolicited offer.

Pros	Cons
• Higher price (highest of the options) • More cash up front • Walk away faster • Stability of deal terms • Business refresh (growth, new energy) • Cost-effective • Breaks deadlock at management level with family	• Long process (9-12 months) • Distraction / loss of focus • Privacy concerns • Emotional for owner • After sale tie-downs • Highest absolute cost of options (but higher benefit) • Complex: involves about 1,000 professional hours • Can be difficult to close

Recapitalization

Finding new ways to "fund the company's balance sheet." Essentially brings in a lender or equity investor to act as a partner in the business. Can sell minority or majority position.

Pros	Cons
• Allows partial exit • Reduces owner risk—diversifies asset concentration • Provides growth capital • Second bite at the apple • Works well with other exit options	• Continuing accountability to partners (not a clean break) • Loss of control • Culture shift • May be slower • Expensive relative to benefit

Orderly Liquidation

The business is shut down through a simple, quick process. Makes sense if asset values exceed the ability of the business to produce income required to support an investment.

Pros	Cons
• Good option when asset value exceeds value of going concern • Sum of the parts is greater than the whole (asset division produces value) • Efficient way to exit • May be less expensive than some of the other options	• Uncertain proceeds—no guarantee • No money for goodwill • Emotional—stigma? • Hard to predict costs • Damage to employees/jobs/community • Higher tax (C-corporations)

KEEP/GROW—ADVANCED VALUE ACCELERATION

If you choose to continue down the path of growing value, you will enter the stage of Advanced Value Acceleration (AVA). In AVA, you will invest more money into the business and increase your personal risk, so consider this carefully. Remember, once you sink the money into AVA, you will need to give your investment time to reach its full return. If you recall our initial list of actions, we sorted them into strategic versus non-strategic. It is in AVA that we begin to take on strategic actions. These are things like:

- Hiring key talent
- Investing in new equipment
- Expanding a facility
- Re-engineering a manufacturing or distribution process
- Engaging in a longer-term customer service or product initiative
- Diversifying your customer base
- Moving into new markets
- Making and integrating an acquisition

In AVA, you take on more risk and usually more debt. When Flexalloy invested in new technology, it was a long-term operational and customer investment. Although we were able to implement in a relatively short period of time, the long-term payback would be years down the road. Even though the cash flow was not immediate, we still were adding considerable value through the increase in customer, human, structural, and social capital.

You use the same process to implement strategic actions as you do with non-strategic/de-risking actions in the Prepare Stage. The difference is that your projects will be bigger and longer-term. You will use the same system by breaking these big projects into 90-day sprints and 30-day (or less) milestones.

In determining your personal and business actions, perhaps you will decide to include one strategic and four non-strategic. Or perhaps, if you really want to go all-out, and have already made significant progress on de-risking, you may only take on one action instead of five. You will use all the things you have already established as your guides: your vision, your SWOT, your core values, your long-term targets, and your brand promise. These will act as your North Star to guide you in making the right choices. By this time, you will have completed at least 10 personal actions (within two sprints), which will provide you the guidance to determine if you are personally committed to these long-term investments. Do you have enough passion? Do you still believe in your vision? Are you willing to assume additional risk? Have you put aside enough financial assets so that you are personally secure?

Hopefully, you have developed or acquired the talent you need to be successful. You have made your systems, processes, and technology more efficient so that they are prepared to scale with the positive changes that will come. Congratulations! You have accomplished all this in the first two cycles of Value Acceleration; you are now ready to go after exponential growth.

SECTION FOUR

Walking to Destiny

In this section, I will describe the six immediate next steps to take action, get educated, build your team, and ultimately, change your outcome.

CHAPTER THIRTEEN

Changing Your Outcome

What is your destiny as a business owner?

I do not believe that our destiny was to simply own a business, despite the magnitude of that undertaking. However, by the very act of starting this entrepreneurial lifestyle, you secured your imminent walk toward certain destiny. So where are you headed? **Your eventual exit.** All things have a beginning and an end, and it is every business owner's reality to eventually transition the business they built. And I am here to tell you that **your destiny is to cash in and to ultimately empower the next generation of ownership**—whether that be one of your children, your employees, management, or some third party you don't even know right now. Your destiny is to leave a legacy, stretching far beyond the present and into a future that is better because of your achievements and contribution. Wallace Wattles believed that the best way to help others and show gratitude was to get rich and give back. I absolutely agree. And

Walking In My Destiny
Malcolm Williams

He has purpose and He has plans for you
To bring you to your expected end
It's a process but one He'll take with you
And He'll lead you to your expected end

You can't imagine you cannot see
The things that He's has just for me
I'm ready to live in prosperity
Walking in my destiny

I named this Value Acceleration business book ***Walking to Destiny*** because it literally explains the truths you must adopt to achieve your well-deserved destiny.

SIX STEPS ON YOUR WALK TO DESTINY

To begin your walk, first you need to own it. Accept your responsibility. Choose the three legs to be the three pillars of your future. Make them your center. Make harvesting your business value your purpose. Organize your entire life, including your business, around these pillars. Own it.

Second, take action now! **Change your paradigm and bring exit planning into the present.** Take the first step of Value Acceleration by completing the Triggering Event. Know your baseline. Understand where you currently benchmark so you can start building transferable value while empowering the next generation of owners, creating your legacy.

Third, truly adopt Value Acceleration as your management and life planning system. Start running your business on the framework outlined in this book. Every single day. Bring your personal goals and aspirations in line with your business aspirations. Doing this will give you a framework for relentless execution of your plan.

Fourth, get yourself educated. Use the educational resources (including those described below) to get on top of this process and steer your path. Reading this book was a key step. Another read that should be high on your list, one of my favorite books of all time: *The Seven Habits of Highly Effective People* by Dr. Stephen Covey. My favorite part of that book is the P/PC principle. "P" stands for productivity. "PC" stands for productive capacity. In the book, Covey asserts that your P and PC need to be in balance. In order to produce well and consistently, you need to invest in your ability to produce. In other words, you need to invest in yourself first. If you don't feed the goose who is laying the golden eggs, the goose will stop laying altogether. Setting time aside to invest in your education, your health, and your spirituality is a PC activity and is vital to your ultimate success.

Fifth, surround yourself with a stellar team and demand better team play. Your teams must be collaborative, accessible, and transparent. Discourage silos. To be effective, you and your core team need to organize around a common organizing principle, which is the **Three Legs of the Stool.** Don't go it alone. You must engage the talent around you to be successful. You must demand that your team put you and your family at the center, and demand that they work together for one purpose: to ensure your legacy and help you monetize your well-deserved riches. The ultimate measure of the team's success is value. Value is achieved by the accomplishment of actions.

Finally, prove your commitment by establishing an investment in Value Acceleration. It should literally be a line item on your budget. That directly communicates your present willingness to invest in the future of your business. Failure is found when your actions don't match your values. Investing time is not enough; you will need to invest some money into this process. Accept that. Bringing in the expertise needed will get you over the hump, keep you focused, and pay dividends far exceeding the costs.

TAKE OWNERSHIP, GET EDUCATED

Transition success rates are poor for many reasons, but a fundamental one is lack of exit planning and business transition education. You don't know what you don't know. So in ignorant bliss, you make assumptions that exit is something you take care of down the road.

The first thing you need to do is accept the importance of exit planning and bring it into the present. Take responsibility. A good way to start is getting yourself educated. The EPI *State of Owner Readiness Survey* reported that 66% of the owners surveyed had not completed any education related to their exit. Is it any wonder you are confused and view the process as future-based, complicated, and time consuming? But are you really going to outsource what is likely to be the largest wealth creation event of your life? The good news is there are a number of resources available to you.

ADVISORS

You can and should contact a credentialed subject matter expert, such as a Certified Exit Planning Advisor® (CEPA®), in your area. These advisors have completed EPI's MBA-style credentialing program. A CEPA can meet with you to discuss the process, answer your questions, and conduct a Triggering Event. You will learn more about your business value than you may have ever been able to assess previously. From there, your CEPA will be able to support you, quarterback your team, oversee your de-risking and growth projects, and secure the business legacy you deserve.

The CEPA Program, created in 2007, was developed by nationally recognized experts in the field of exit planning and is based within the Value Acceleration Methodology. Today, there are more than 600 credentialed CEPA advisors worldwide. Those who hold the CEPA designation are CPAs and accountants, financial planners and wealth managers, attorneys, commercial lenders, insurance advisors, M&A advisors and business brokers, and management consultants who have gone the extra mile to learn how to do this right for the business owners they serve.

Most CEPAs operate right here in the U.S., and there is likely at least one in your local community. Go to the EPI website (www.Exit-Planning-Institute.org) and search for a CEPA in your area. Or call the headquarters office for a referral. My team will gladly get you an introduction to a top-notch advisor at no cost. The CEPA is a critical advisor for Value Acceleration and someone who belongs at the head of your team.

When you meet with an advisor who claims to be an expert in exit planning, please make sure they are credentialed. Plainly, there are a lot of hacks out there who claim to be exit planners. Ask them how long they have been working with business owners. Investigate their reputation. What credentials do they hold? Are they experienced in dealing with the problems and challenges of business owners? Do they understand the conflicts that arise as a result of conflicting manager, family, and owner values? Can they speak in detail about the key drivers of value and embrace a focus on value and income? Do they take a holistic view of exit planning, not just a functional view? What methodology do they use (or do they even have one)? Ask them to share stories and results from past engagements. Having a CEPA at your table will directly enhance your knowledge and acumen.

ASSOCIATIONS AND PEER GROUPS

Since 2005, the Exit Planning Institute has pioneered the exit planning industry and is fully dedicated to serving the educational and resource needs of credentialed exit planning professionals. Uniquely, EPI is a cross-functional group. Our mission is to change the outcome for business owners and their families by helping them identify, protect, build, harvest, and manage their business value. There are resources available from EPI geared toward you and other owners, like the *State of Owner Readiness Survey,* national *Certificate in Exit Planning Workshops,* and regional *Owners Forums.* You do not need to be a member or working with a CEPA to participate. A major focus for EPI is bringing awareness to owners like you. So you are encouraged to utilize these opportunities for training and education.

In addition to EPI, there are many associations that are dedicated to helping you. Look into the Family Firm Institute (FFI). FFI is primarily dedicated to educating and supporting family business advisors, but you don't have to be an advisor to attend their conferences. If you want to get some solid education on family business and the same educational exposure your advisors are receiving, attend one of their conferences. I recommend attending these conferences with your entire family.

Plan to attend an ESOP (Employee Stock Ownership Plan) conference. Look for a local organization that provides support to business owners interested in selling to employees. In Northeast Ohio, we have a wonderful group called the Ohio Employee Ownership Center (OEOC), a nonprofit, that is affiliated with Kent State University. There are similar groups nationwide, so see what you can learn there.

Many trade associations and peer groups are now addressing the exit planning phenomenon, offering education and peer group support to their members. Vistage International and Entrepreneurs Organization are two options that come to mind.

Many local and national universities have "Centers for Family Business." Case Western Reserve University, again here in Cleveland, has a great family business center. So do the University of San Francisco and the University of Chicago. Finding one near you is as simple as going to the website of your local university and checking to see if they are hosting programs that you might attend. That's a no-brainer.

Many local communities offer education through their economic development offices or Chambers of Commerce. Economic Development groups all over the country are realizing the importance of ensuring the continuity of privately held businesses in their communities. Several of the more progressive ones are becoming CEPAs and offering local and statewide services to their business markets.

Look for a local EPI Chapter in your area. We have an expanding network of chapters in many cities throughout the U.S. and Australia. We have chapters in New York City; Atlanta; Chicago; Northeast Ohio; St. Louis; Indianapolis; North Texas; Northern and Southern California; Salt Lake City; Minneapolis; Southern Nevada; Phoenix; and Sydney,

Australia. Every chapter has unique aspects related to its local culture and business environment. The chapters work on a common framework built by EPI and apply that framework to the specific local needs of the regions they serve. Each has a president who is a thought leader on this subject and a leadership team to develop curriculum to educate the local community of advisors and business owners.

The chapters hold regular education and networking events throughout the year. Business owners are welcome to attend these chapter events. Many of them now host annual, semiannual, or quarterly Owners Forums where local business owners can interact with credentialed advisors, participate in educational seminars and breakout sessions with other business owners, and listen and learn from nationally recognized subject matter experts on identifying, protecting, building, harvesting, and managing business value, family business ownership, master planning, strategic planning, marketing, information technology, talent acquisition, retention, and management.

Furthermore, CEPAs in these communities may offer small peer group roundtables and seminars which benefit and educate owners. My firm has partnered with a leading CPA firm in town called Skoda Minotti. This is a CPA firm that gets it. In my opinion, a big reason they "get it" is because the firm was founded and is still presently led by Greg Skoda, an entrepreneur first, CPA second; and a progressive partner in the firm named Mike Trabert. Mike, a CEPA, has taken on the challenge of educating the other partners and bringing proactive Value Acceleration solutions to Skoda's client base.

ASPIRE PLUS OWNER ROUNDTABLES

You should find a local provider of Aspire Plus Owner Roundtables (these are the Roundtables I have referenced throughout this book). They are delivered in a five-part series, teaching the Five Stages of the Value Maturity. It's one two-hour session each month for five months straight. You will attend these sessions in groups of eight to 12 business owners. This forms a peer group that goes through the education together, sharing your challenges, points of view, and real-life stories with each other. It is a perfect forum for learning what you don't know. For example, I asked one of the owners in an interview to rate on a scale of one to six (one being "I know little to nothing;" six being "I am an expert") how well she thought she understood business valuation. She answered,

> *"Before attending the Roundtables, I was maybe a two. After, I feel I am a five."*

Another owner commented that he wished he had been through the series 10 years ago. He noted that if he had, he would have approached things in his business differently the last 10 years, saying:

> *"I wish I had those 10 years back..."*

One hundred percent of owners who have completed the Roundtable series indicated they would recommend the program to fellow business owners, with survey comments saying:

- "I'm not much for seminars. Time is in short supply to begin with. But this was absolutely worth it."
- "The courses provide specific and actionable information that was directly applicable to the management of our business and

understanding its value quantitatively and qualitatively."
- "This program allowed me to better understand how to grow the value of my organization and to provide a framework for ongoing value improvement."
- "While I view myself as being experienced in and knowledgeable about many of the topics covered by the Roundtable, the approach to many of the topics provides me a totally new perspective, as well as an actionable framework to assist my company, my partners, and me as we consider a few topics the Roundtables covered."

To put it into perspective, these owners spent only 10 hours over five months to achieve this benefit. Again, a no-brainer for your value growth educational pursuits.

> *Don't want to do all this legwork to find these groups and programs? Easy: call a CEPA.*

CEPAs are familiar with all the programs in your community and many of the advisors: both the good ones and the hacks. They can tee you up with the right resources. They have your best interests at heart. They have invested their time and money to learn how to do it right. And they will help develop an educational platform for you and provide invaluable guidance on your journey.

MANUFACTURERS, FRANCHISORS, AND BIG CORPORATIONS

If you are a manufacturer or franchisor who sells through distributors, dealers, or franchisees, or you are a big corporation who buys products and services from middle market privately held businesses, you would be wise to offer succession planning and value acceleration education programs to your supply chain partners. It will take some coordination, but not much money, to offer this as a value-added service. And it may very well save your supply chain.

In the case I discussed in Chapter Two, the manufacturer provided me a platform and paid a reasonable fee for me to speak at their national conference. Then they provided a facility where we could gather with their dealers, and their families, over a day and a half, to teach them in a very interactive setting about exit planning and value acceleration. Each dealer paid a small registration fee (albeit a substantially discounted fee relative to market value) to attend the program. The manufacturer was not looking to make money on the program, simply to cover the cost of having me and Peter Christman come in to teach. Their event broke even, but the benefits? Tremendous. Below are some of the comments made by the attendees to the vice president of sales who hosted the workshop:

Thank you for the kind words and taking time to send them to me. I came back with newfound enthusiasm. I wrote a contingency plan, organized a board of advisers both for the business and personally for Rachelle should something happen to me. Sunbelt will be doing a business evaluation next Tuesday and I have both a financial planner and CPA and both are on the advisory board. Rather than writing processes for individual departments and personnel, I have contracted a video production company to assist in recording systems where they will be placed in the cloud on SF....employees, new hires, and management will have PW access, which will be measurable, as when they view or review, their access is documented. On another topic...why the h*** do you do this stuff in Cleveland in February? —Waukesha, WI

Best meeting he has ever attended. Hired an evaluator and accountant. He is going through his entire business, line by line, and making changes. Calls me every few days to give me an update. —Claire, MI

Calls me every few days to ask questions. He and Joy loved the meeting. He is hiring an evaluator and has met with his partners to develop a buy-out plan for the future.
—Harrisonburg, VA

Called just to thank me for having the meeting (he gives me far too much credit). Said it was a fantastic meeting and that he is looking at his business totally differently.
—Walnut Creek, CA

> *She called to thank us for holding the meeting. Last week, she removed some weak links in her dealership (which I thought she would never do) to improve her business. She even told me that she does not know what we told Luanne, but she likes what she is doing!* —Meadville, PA

> *He is starting the process of hiring an attorney to set up a succession plan to sell the business to his daughter and son-in-law.* —Pittsburgh, PA

These owners spent a day and a half, only about 12 hours, to get this kind of benefit. And they were even willing to come to Cleveland in February to get it!

My point with these examples is to show you that quality educational resources are available today to help you, and if you spend just a little bit of your time to learn about what exit planning really is, you can begin to change your outcome.

START READING

In addition to attending seminars and conferences and speaking with advisors in this space, another really simple way to start getting educated is to start reading. If you are reading this sentence, you are already off to a very good start. The subject of exit planning, succession planning, transition planning (whatever you want call it these days) is a hot topic and the industry is starting to produce some pretty decent literature. For a list of recommended reading, visit my website, www.SniderValueIndex.com.

COMPLETE THE TRIGGERING EVENT

As I described in the Five Stages of Value Maturity, the very first step in Value Acceleration is to Identify Value by completing the Triggering Event. This step is always first and can't be skipped because it sets the baseline for measuring value (and everyone's performance going forward). If you do nothing else, complete this step. If, after the Triggering Event, you don't feel compelled to proceed, then stop. You would fall into the 30% of owners who don't want to approach Value Acceleration. But odds are, you are in the 70% and you will have several "a-ha" moments, seeing and deeply understanding, for the first time, things about business value and how your personal aspirations impact it. Knowledge is power. Get a clear view of your business. That clarity is a standalone benefit.

ESTABLISH YOUR TEAM

Surround yourself with A-players. Remember "First Who, Then What." Exiting properly is complicated. Sorry, that's just the way it is. You might have dozens of team members. As such, it is vital that this team works well together, yet rarely is that so.

You need to own this team and be the team leader. You and your family need to be at the center. This is by far your largest financial asset, and as I have indicated in previous chapters, this effort is more than just monetizing your largest financial asset—it is likely to be the love of your life. This is one of the reasons you start by investing time in getting educated and adopting a framework. A lot of different people will move in and out of the framework on your walk to destiny. You don't want to allow them to buffalo you. And you absolutely need to make clear that the final decisions are yours. Remember that each team member will be looking at things from their functional point of view. Overall, that is healthy, if managed by you.

Your attorney looks to keep you out of trouble. Your CPA has an aversion to risk. Your financial planner wants hit a certain rate of return (and they would also love to get their hands on more of your wealth). Family members and partners can have good intentions, and sometimes hidden agendas. Your Value Advisor is okay with calculated risks—but with your money, not theirs.

All that being said, I am generalizing and probably not being completely fair to them. But the point is, you want to consider their advice, but benchmark it against your own educated vision. Don't let any one of them take over control of the team or manipulate you into doing what's best for them, rather than you. If your team can't come to a consensus when the time comes to make a decision, you make it. You choose. If your team is consistently struggling to come to a consensus, then you probably have the wrong team.

There is likely to be some overlap, but you are going to basically need two core teams because you will be walking to destiny on two concurrent paths: personal and business. Your personal team (the Inner Circle) will be helping you execute your personal actions and the other will be helping you execute your business actions. These teams will include your family members and partners, your key management and employees, suppliers and customers, and your core and secondary advisors. Let's start with the one I think you most fear (and many of you just hate): your advisor team.

WHY DO YOU HATE ADVISORS? YOU HAVE YOUR REASONS.

For one, they each have very different roles and their advice can be conflicting and expensive. Yet they all covet that direct relationship with you. They all want to achieve that "trusted advisor" status. Besides giving them a more predictable stream of income from you, their client, it also gives them more meaning. Most owners hate consultants. However, most advisors, despite what you might think, genuinely want to help you. They take great pride and satisfaction in doing well by their clients and seeing their clients succeed and be happy. If you view advisors as "evil" in your mind, I'd argue they are a necessary evil.

Advisors tend to be very technical people and like control. Anything that separates them from that is a threat. I can remember speaking with the partner of a CPA firm who had been providing accounting services for years to a new client of mine. I had recently been hired to perform a valuation for the client. I had not previously worked with this CPA firm and no one there was a CEPA or member of EPI. So I set up a meeting with a partner of the firm to introduce myself, share our methodology, get his insights, and begin the process of establishing a relationship. The conversation went something like this:

Chris: I have been hired by the client to complete an assessment and valuation of the business.

CPA: Oh really? I hadn't been told that.

Chris: Well, I think you know they are thinking about exiting and they spoke to their attorney, John, and he recommended they meet with me. John and I have worked together before. You know John, right?

CPA: Well, of course, John and I go way back. Frankly, I'm surprised he didn't call to let me know about this.

Chris: I'm sure he intended to or will. We met with the clients last week and went over our approach. They really liked it and wanted to get started right away. Since we haven't met, and I know how strongly they view their relationship with you, I wanted to reach out and introduce myself, share our approach, and see what insights and advice you might want to share. I want to do a really good job for them and I really believe in working as a team. It's one of our core principles as CEPAs. As the team leader, I realize the importance of getting everyone's input and points of view.

CPA: Team leader? What do you mean by that?

Chris: One of the roles of a Value Advisor is to help coordinate all the resources that are needed to successful go through the process. For the other advisors on the team, I help them get engaged and help them resolve issues.

CPA: Hmmm, I thought that's what I did.

And there you have it. Off to a great start—not! No offense intended to CPAs, but the less progressive ones can be the worst about having control issues. As a side note to the owners reading this book: this is why, if possible, you want to have as many CEPAs on the team as possible. I am not claiming all CEPAs are perfect. But I can tell you that CEPAs have been educated and credentialed on the importance of working in teams. As the owner and leader of the team, it would be wise for you to meet with your advisor team and (1) explain to them the role of the CEPA, (2) state that the CEPA is not a threat, and (3) communicate that the CEPA will enhance everyone's role in the process. This is helpful when it comes directly from you.

One of the biggest frustrations I hear from owners is "my advisors don't work as a team. My CPA says one thing, my attorney another, and my financial planner something else. I don't know who to believe. They all think they know better than me and they can't seem to get on the same page. I find the whole thing extremely frustrating. All I see are big dollar signs for their services. If they can't get on the same page, how are they supposed to help me?"

Instead of taking action and demanding this change, many of you stick your head in the sand. One of the big problems, historically, for many owners is the limited ability to measure the impact of all these fees: What's the ROI?

It can be difficult to measure the value-add of advisors. Using value as the measurement provides a baseline for the entire team, including the family, management, and employees. If you use the value of the business and an integrated project plan that synchronizes these activities with the creation of value, you will be much more open to the idea of using outside advisors. In many cases, advisors are their own worst enemy because they don't work together on a common framework. Instead, they compete with each other for a percentage of the money you are reluctantly willing to spend on professional services.

At the beginning of your value growth effort, hold a team meeting with your core advisors after completing the Triggering Event to review the results of the personal, financial, and business assessments and correlation to value to solicit input and ideas. Doing this is usually enough to calm everyone down. And do the same thing with your board of advisors—or even better, bring them all in one night after work and make the Triggering Event deliverable the focal point of your next board meeting. After all, it will become the basis for measuring your success going forward. Shouldn't all your primary stakeholders and key advisors be given the opportunity to understand where we are and where we intend to go? They are all here for the single purpose of helping you be successful. Plus, many of them depend on your success.

All advisors should be reviewed periodically to ensure their services are relevant and contributing to the increasing value of your business. Sometimes the business outgrows the advisors that were relevant in the past. You may still have the business attorney from when you started the business and she may still be giving you solid business advice. But if you have decided to sell your business, you will need an attorney who understands mergers and acquisitions. Your best buddy from grade school might be managing your investment portfolio because you trust him, but is he best suited to guide you in harvesting the value of the business and managing that value, often five times your present net worth?

THE CORE TEAM

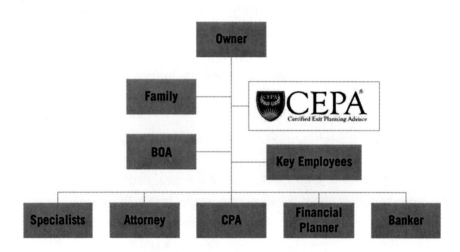

Exhibit FF: Exit Planning Ecosystem

Your core team should include your attorney, CPA, financial planner, banker, and Value Advisor (who should hold the CEPA credential). In fact, the more CEPAs, the better. In addition, you should have a board of advisors, or perhaps a board of directors, and should consider a family council and/or an employee/management council as members of the core team. This is even more important if you are considering a family, management, or employee transition option. Beyond that, all kinds of different specialists may be required depending on which gate of Value Acceleration you are in.

For now, let's explore the teams that you need. Your **core team** will be with you all the way through.

FINANCIAL PLANNER OR WEALTH MANAGER

Your financial planner or wealth manager is a critical pick. Yet, this pick is often overlooked and underestimated. So choose your financial planner or wealth manager carefully. I like to get a financial planner involved right from the beginning, for all the financial reasons I have noted elsewhere in this book. We need to get busy building a portfolio outside the business and looking at getting the right tax, estate, and insurance planning in place. These strategies can take years to fully implement—often three to seven, in fact—so we need to get started with these right away if they are missing.

Beyond that, the financial planner or wealth manager (I am implying the same role, although they are not the same thing) is the person who can tell me what kind of position the owner and owner's family are in personally. Are they financially in good shape outside the business? Do they need the income from the business? What would happen if they were to lose this income, die, become disabled, or become unable to work anymore? What if there was a divorce that would force them to split up the assets? If they have a business partner, what if there's a falling out? What if they were to lose their largest customer or a key employee, or face a significant environmental, safety, or legal issue? How much do they need to support their lifestyle? What are their spending habits like? Are there any special-needs children we have to think about? Are there health issues we need to plan for? Are there seniors in the family that they may need to support with assisted living, health care, or home health care? What are their children's educational requirements? Have they been planned for? What is their risk profile? And on and on.

The financial planner will ask these questions and provide alternatives and answers. These answers are vital to the rest of the team. We don't want to be recommending the owner invest in the business, taking on more leverage and risk, if they have not done the basic things necessary to protect what they already have—especially if there are special needs outside the business. And once this is all said and done and you exit the business, everyone else goes away except the financial planner. Maybe the attorney hangs around for some estate planning or small legal matters you might need. But you are going to rely on the financial planner to manage your nest egg once you leave the business. The rest of us will be on to the next assignment helping someone else identify, protect, build, harvest, and manage their wealth.

ATTORNEY

The best attorneys are business advisors first, like mine, Hal Maxfield of Cavitch, Familo, & Durkin. Your attorney is not just there to bail you out of problems, intimidate rogue employees and people who want sue you, challenge other board members, and resolve family disputes. Your attorney is, hopefully, someone who has worked in dozens, if not hundreds, of family-owned businesses. You need to allow your attorney to really to get under the hood with you and understand your core business operations and personal aspirations. A good attorney will not know everything you need. But they will know who to call and are likely to have the specialist, be that an estate planner, litigator, or pension plan specialist, that you will need on this journey.

And please understand, they are not God. Everything they say is not always the definitive or the right call. It may be legally correct, but it may not be best business advice considering the entire picture. No offense intended to attorneys. I have many friends who are attorneys. We have three attorneys in my immediate family (and that's plenty). I love them and we all need them. But they are not all-knowing. There are attorneys who get things done and attorneys who will never allow you to get anything done. Find one who really understands business. Take their advice. But make your own decisions.

CPA

A CPA who is not afraid to lose your business is absolutely essential. I mention not being afraid to lose your business for a reason. Too many CPAs do not want you to exit, as they are afraid they will lose you as a customer who provides a very valuable recurring revenue stream to them. Today, this is changing as progressive firms like Skoda Minotti, headquartered in Cleveland, realize that exit planning and value acceleration will provide a new revenue stream for them and it is their duty to have your best interest at heart. The CPA industry is consolidating. One reason is that the CPA industry is facing what all owners are facing: aging Baby Boomers who are looking at retirement.

The CPA holds the gold medal for advisor status with business owners. This person is the most trusted advisor. In the EPI *State of Owner Readiness Survey,* we asked business owners who was their most trusted advisor. The CPA came out twice as high as the second runner up. And who do you think was runner up, as the second most trusted advisor? The spouse. That's right. In our survey, your CPA was trusted twice as much as your spouse. Now if that isn't an advisor gold medal, I'm not sure what is.

Your CPA will be involved in assessing and valuing the business. They will help you clean up (if needed) and maintain your financial records. They may help you with project planning and execution. They are involved in every stage of value creation. Many firms today offer far more than just traditional CPA-type accounting work. Many have become services clearing houses with the ability to offer an array of services including financial planning, insurance, pension planning, HR, marketing, IT, and (you guessed it) exit planning.

I believe the CPA firms are the farthest along in developing their exit planning services. At EPI, they make up a third of our entire membership base and represent some of our greatest leaders. No doubt, they can be too technical sometimes, but they do have arguably the best grasp of the tax numbers, combined with good background and training to help you succeed with exit planning.

THE BANKER

When my son started his first business (which he later successfully sold to a strategic buyer at the age of 24), my father gave him this advice: "As a businessman, your most important relationship is with your banker."

Most owners don't think about the banker when they think of exiting. Part of the problem is that many bankers do not develop a relationship with the owner outside of their banking needs. They also are subject to heavy regulation, which limits the types of services they can provide you. However, one of the questions we ask in our business assessment is: How strong is your relationship with your bank?

Surprisingly, many owners rate this relationship low. They only go to the bank when they need money or when they have to explain a variance to the covenants they agreed to when they borrowed money from the bank.

This is really a missed opportunity. The owner should try to talk to their banker monthly, keeping the banker informed of how the business is doing, good or bad; sharing his aspirations with the banker; and letting the banker take a look at the numbers.

The banker should absolutely be involved in your exit plan. For one, if you, your children, employees, management, partner, or an outside buyer need money to finance your exit, your existing banker is likely to be the first one to step up, assuming you have kept him or her abreast of your plan. They know the business and its quirks, positive and negative. They don't want to lose that business. They are, after all, in the business of lending money. If they are kept apprised and are permitted to provide you with some advice to position the business and your successor to be in a better position to secure the financing you need to execute your succession plan, they are more likely to back you.

FAMILY

Certain family members should be part of your core team, such as your spouse and some of the children. Some owners will set up a family council which acts similar to a business board of advisors. A family council can help manage the collisions between the business and family dynamics discussed earlier.

As Richard Jackim and Peter Christman wrote in *The $10 Trillion Opportunity,* "…a family council protects the growth, development, and welfare of the family itself…it provides family members with a regular structured forum to communicate, voice concerns, have input, and participate in determining how to deal with business issues…with this structure, the family does not feel obliged to pack the corporate board with family members." I recommend that at least one family member act as a liaison to the board of advisors.

BOARD OF ADVISORS

Some companies, depending on their structure, are required to have a board of directors. The board of directors does not necessarily perform the same role as a board of advisors. If set up correctly, the board of advisors will provide the owner and family members with valuable advice from individuals with years of experience of working with other businesses, both corporate and family. They can help you sort out and vet succession candidates, including possible family members; and recruit, motivate, retain, and evolve talent. They will help provide oversight of your Master Plan, and most of all, hold you, the owner, accountable.

One of the common owner problems is that you are not accountable to anyone. You are at the very top. Inside employees and management are squeamish to tell you what you need to hear. Even long-time advisors awkwardly hesitate when telling you what you need to hear, for fear of losing you as a client.

As a board member and mentor to many children who work in their father's or mother's business, I can tell you that sometimes these family members need help communicating with (and managing) Mom and Dad. They fear saying what they want and need to say to you, out of respect, and would prefer to avoid dysfunction in the family. A solid board of advisors can provide a mechanism for brutal honesty and accountability.

There are many other roles an outside board of advisors can fill. Below is a sample list of these pulled from *The $10 Trillion Opportunity:*

- Reviewing financial statements and audits
- Reviewing corporate mission and strategy
- Reviewing and approving budgets

- Monitoring business performance
- Monitoring business goals
- Making recommendations regarding major capital expenditures
- Assessing organizational structure and policies
- Approving mergers and acquisitions
- Approving major debt transactions

Establishing or assessing the need for an outside board of advisors is usually one of the first things you will do in the first 90-day cycle of Value Acceleration (during the Prepare Stage in Gate Two).

KEY EMPLOYEES

Sometimes putting key employees on your core team is appropriate, especially if you have already designated a successor. Giving them the opportunity to interact with the rest of your core team is a great way to vet them and teach them what it's like to be at the helm of the ship. It also allows them to express their points of view on strategic matters and own the execution of the plan. And it reassures and builds confidence with all the other stakeholders.

SECONDARY TEAM MEMBERS AND STAKEHOLDERS

As if your core team members were not enough, many other specialists will need to interact with your core team through the process. You may need functional specialists such as customer service, marketing, manufacturing, operations, distribution, finance, legal, HR, and accounting. When considering options, you will need to interact with outside option specialists like investment bankers and M&A intermediaries, private equity and family offices; and inside transition specialists including ESOP specialist, family transition specialists, and attorneys who are experienced in management and partner buy-outs. You may need to consult with specific lenders who provide capital funding and mezzanine lending.

You shouldn't neglect other stakeholders like customers, suppliers, employees, and the local community—all of whom contribute and depend on your success.

THE ROLE OF THE "VALUE ADVISOR"

EPI has defined the role of your team leader, or quarterback, as the Value Advisor™. The Value Advisor is a trusted advisor—one of their jobs is to watch your back and help you manage all these relationships, all of which are critical components to your success.

I chose the phrase *Value Advisor* because this person's primary objective is to help you grow value and unlock the wealth trapped in your business. The official Value Advisor is a new position in the industry. They typically have a background as a CPA, financial planner, or management consultant, or frankly, former business owner, because they need to understand the game of business, its processes and functions, and the numbers involved. But again, let's be clear, this is a separate role from those primary specialties. For example, you shouldn't hold the roles of Value Advisor *and* CPA at the same time. These are separate and distinct responsibilities.

This is why the fees are separate and incremental. The key justification for the incremental fees is the accelerated value and operating income that results from the implementation of the Value Advisor's projects and their structured, collaborative role in helping you manage these vital relationships.

Many think of the role of the Value Advisor as the quarterback of the stakeholder team. Just like on a football field, none of the other players on the offense "report" to the quarterback. But when the quarterback calls the play, everyone on that field has a role and job to do. The better they synchronize their efforts, the more effective they will be. Sometimes they get smashed. However, if you have the right people in the right roles, you usually score more often than the other guy.

Often, the success of the team is dependent on the strength of the quarterback. Just look at the success of the New England Patriots with Tom Brady or the Denver Broncos with Peyton Manning. Although quarterbacks, at least the effective ones, are able to call audibles, they follow and execute a game plan. They are often involved in developing that game plan. However, the most effective teams are able to adjust their execution during the game to exploit weaknesses and opportunities presented by the other team or offset what the other team has figured out about their game plan.

The quarterback of your stakeholder team is no different. You need someone to lead. As the owner, you certainly don't have the time and, frankly, you don't have the experience. You need a playbook and game plan, which are developed in Gate One. You execute your plan in Gate Two. You recalibrate during the game every 90 days to execute more effectively. You benefit in the end in Gate Three, either accelerating to the championship or exiting and entering the business hall of fame.

WHAT DOES A VALUE ADVISOR DO?

An easy way to articulate the role of a Value Advisor is to think of them as a project manager. They are managing the project of unlocking your business wealth by helping you identify, protect, build, harvest, and manage the value of your business. The Value Advisor will:

- Assess your personal, financial, and business situation and correlate this to the value of your business.
- Develop a scorecard and be able to quantitatively and qualitatively measure the impact from the implementation of personal, financial, and business actions which are driving up the value of the business.
- Develop a plan with sequential steps and milestones and identify the critical path.
- Define the deliverables to be produced at each milestone and gate.
- Solicit help and input from others on the team.
- Establish communication protocols.
- Facilitate communication, resolve issues, and hold people accountable for deliverables.
- Keep things on track and on budget.

I think it was all of the project management work I did over the years implementing systems and processes and working as a true change agent that really prepared me for my Value Advisor role and to be the leader of the stakeholder team. At Price Waterhouse, I constantly faced the challenge of selling the role of the project manager to executives.

"What do they actually do?" the executives would ask. I would ask the executive, "How badly do you want to get this done?" The executive would say, "It's paramount—we need to make sure, given all the investment and time we are going to spend, that it gets done."

"Well, then, hiring a project manager to ensure that happens is the difference between getting it done and not getting it done. You need a specialist on the team who understands how to get things done. That's what the project manager does. You need to create a line item in your budget for this and think of it as part of the overall cost of the project and return on investment."

The stakes were often very high. We were implementing big, expensive, culture-changing, multi-year projects for these companies. Is your exit any different? Nope. An exit strategy is a big, expensive, culture- changing, multi-year project and it requires a seasoned and credentialed leader to get it done right.

Most of the time, the Value Advisor role is vacant. If it is filled, it's often filled with someone who does not really understand the role of a being project manager or the holistic approach you have learned in this book. That's doing you a disservice and creates more issues than it resolves. It requires you to spend more money than you should. And circling all the way back, I believe that is a big reason you hate consultants.

The Value Advisor is the most qualified advisor to fulfill this missing role and takes that monkey off your back. The only way to move toward becoming a credentialed Value Advisor is to start by getting your CEPA credential from EPI.

WHAT SKILLS DOES A VALUE ADVISOR NEED TO BE EFFECTIVE?

A Value Advisor is a change agent that aligns the Three Legs of the Stool. In addition to project management skills, Value Advisors need to demonstrate empathetic understanding of business ownership. They need to be able to reach the owner personally. They need to be able to dissect and analyze financial statements and the financial, cultural, and personal consequences of both strategic direction and daily decisions. Skills in change management and collaboration are very important. Knowledge of who and when to bring someone in and who to use is important. The

Value Advisor makes sure the process you use to get things done is fast and flexible so that you can respond quickly when the unexpected happens. They also need to be a teacher. They will not only catch fish for you, they will teach your team how to fish so they can do it themselves.

HOW MUCH TIME WILL YOU NEED TO SPEND ON YOUR WALK TO DESTINY?

Cutting through the fat, I've outlined what your investment could look like when taking on Value Acceleration:

Exhibit GG: Value Acceleration Time Investment

		Personal	Business	Total
Mid-Month 1:1 Check-In Workshops	12 mid-months, 2 hours x 5 key people	120	120	240
Monthly Accountability Workshops	2 per quarter w/ teams, assume 3 hours	24	24	48
Quarterly Renewal Workshops	Assume full day, 1 per quarter	32	32	64
Annual Retreat	1 day annually	8	8	16
Monthly Meeting w/ Value Advisor	12 @ 2 hours			24
Education	2 events. 2-3 days in duration annually			48
Total Time Dedicated to Value Acceleration				**440**
Available Hours	Assuming 2,500 hours worked annually			2,500
Percent of available time dedicated to Value Acceleration				18%

Once you have the system rolling, you will need to spend less than 20% of your time on Value Acceleration. This seems to be a reasonable amount of time to spend managing your most significant financial asset. I have budgeted 12 Mid-Month 1:1 Check-In sessions, personal and business, with each of your five core team members. This could be less, but it assumes you have set five personal and five business actions each quarter.

You will have a Monthly Accountability Team Workshop for the first two months of each quarter. The third month of each quarter, you will hold a Quarterly Renewal Workshop. I have also budgeted one day per year for an annual retreat for business and personal, which may include your budgeting process.

To ensure you stay on the same page, you should plan to meet monthly, one-on-one, with your Value Advisor. Work into your budget at least two educational events, such as attending a conference, an Owners Forum, or a Roundtable series in your area. Plan to spend six days per year on education. This totals around 440 hours per year. Assuming you are working at least 2,500 hours per year, or about 50 hours per week, this means you will spend less than 20% of your time managing your personal and business affairs. Again, seems pretty reasonable to me.

CONCLUSION

That's all I have for you. Now it's up to you. You are walking on a path toward your exit. My dream in writing this book was to empower you to unlock the wealth your business has held for you and create the future and legacy you deserve. You can put this book down and do nothing. Or you can get busy. The choice is now yours. Secure your success, alongside other master owners. Discover, prepare, and decide what your walk to destiny will ultimately be. I will end with one more lyric for you:

> *Let Your Light Shine*
> *Keb' Mo'*
>
> *There's something I need to say,*
> *If you could see you,*
> *The way I see you,*
> *You'd start flying on your own.*
>
> *Step on up,*
> **Step into your greatness.**
> *Don't be afraid.*
> *There's a place where you will rise up to;*
> *No one else could do what you do.*
>
> *It's a short ride,*
> *Down a long road.*
> *When the rains come,*
> *And the winds blow,*
> *Let your light shine,*
> *Wherever you go.*

THE END

APPENDIX

EXHIBITS

Page	Exhibits
6	A: Privately Held Businesses in the United States
11	B: 2013 EPI State of Owner Readiness Survey Results Snapshot
13	C: WMFC Generational Differences Chart Excerpt
44	D: Exit Planning Issues
48	E: Owner Paradigm Shift
50	F: Personal Timing Chart
51	G: Business Lifecycle Chart
51	H: Private Capital Market Timing Chart
56	I: Drivers and Influences
73	J: The Five Stages of Value Maturity
75	K: Risk Areas
81	L: Value Maturity Index
88	M: Forbes Top 10 Most Valued Businesses in 2016
89	N: Intangibles versus Tangibles
117	O: Brand Statement
118	P: Degree of Specialization
120	Q: Business Planning Pyramid
135	R: Master Planning
136	S: The Value Acceleration Methodology
138	T: The Guided Discovery Steps & Deliverables
147	U: Strategic Value Simple Math
149	V: Industry Multiples Comparables
152	W: Profit Gap
159	X: Exit Readiness Scorecard
169	Y: Range of Value
169	Z: Value Gap
170	AA: Value Growth Opportunity
183	BB: Setting Priorities

Page	Exhibits
194	CC: Workshops | Not Meetings
206	DD: Sample Quarterly Offsite Agenda
218	EE: Are You Ready? | 10 Things To Determine If You Are
246	FF: Exit Planning Ecosystem
258	GG: Value Acceleration Time Investment

RECOMMENDED READING LIST

Bennis, Warren. *Managing the Dream: Reflections on Leadership and Change.* New York: Perseus Publishing, 2000.

Bossidy, Larry and Ram Charan. *Execution: The Discipline of Getting Things Done.* New York: Crown Business, 2002.

Brown, John H. *How To Run Your Business So You Can Leave It In Style.* Denver: Business Enterprise Press, 1997.

Christman, Peter G. *The Master Plan: Exit Strategy For Successful Business Owners.* 2015.

Collins, Jim and Jerry I. Porras. *Built to Last: Successful Habits of Visionary Companies.* New York: Harper Collins, 2002.

Collins, Jim. *Good to Great.* New York: Harper Collins, 2001.

Covey, Stephen R. *The Seven Habits of Highly Effective People.* New York: Free Press, 1989.

Danco, Léon A. *Beyond Survival: A Guide for Business Owners and Their Families.* Michigan: Reston Pub. Co., 1975.

Deans, Thomas William. *Every Family's Business: 12 Commonsense Questions to Protect Your Wealth.*
Orangeville: Détente Financial Press Ltd., 2013.

Gerber, Michael E. *The E-Myth*. New York: Harper Collins, 1995.

Hams, Brad, with John A. Byrne. *Ownership Thinking*. New York: McGraw-Hill, 2012.

Harnish, Verne. *Mastering the Rockefeller Habits*. New York: SelectBooks, 2002.

Jackim, Richard E. and Peter G. Christman. *The $10 Trillion Opportunity*. Chicago: R. Jackim & Company, 2005.

Stewart, Thomas A. *The Wealth of Knowledge: Intellectual Capital and the Twenty-first Century Organization*. New York: Doubleday, 2001.

Ungashick, Patrick A. *Dance in the End Zone: The Business Owner's Exit Planning Playbook*. Alpharetta: BookLogix, 2013.

Wattles, Wallace D. *The Science of Getting Rich*. Blacksburg: Thrifty Books, 2009.

Welch, Jack. *Jack: Straight from the Gut*. New York: Warner Business Books, 2001.

PUBLIC SPEAKING

Walking to Destiny provides a roadmap and concepts which, when adopted, can increase readiness and attractiveness as business owners approach their exit. Chris Snider delivers keynote speeches, trainings, and workshops surrounding the topics of Master Planning and the Three Legs of the Stool, the Four C's, the Five Stages of Value Maturity, and Relentless Execution. This education is for:

- Top-tier professional advisors and consultants dedicated to helping their clients successfully grow and exit their businesses
- Legal, asset management, and accounting firms committed to successful wealth transfers
- Business owners looking to educate their executives and staff on how to grow value in the business and think like owners
- Community leaders wanting to educate their local business owner market on how to successfully transition their businesses
- Industry associations dedicated to preparing their members for succession
- Financial/professional associations looking to educate their members on how to perform exit planning services
- Entrepreneurs wanting to use exit strategy as a business strategy and stage their company for rapid growth and high market value

For speaking fees and availability, please contact Brooke Norman at (216) 712-4244 or BNorman@Exit-Planning-Institute.org.

Chris Snider is a frequent speaker in Chicago, Cleveland, New York City, San Francisco, San Diego, Las Vegas, Phoenix, Dallas, South Florida, St. Louis, Milwaukee, Atlanta, Los Angeles, and New Orleans. Discounts on travel are available for back-to-back bookings.

VOICE OF THE INDUSTRY

Christopher M. Snider, CEPA, CEO and president of the Exit Planning Institute, creator of the Value Acceleration Methodology™, and managing partner of Snider Premier Growth, is recognized as a thought leader and trendsetter in the field of value acceleration and exit planning. With a message that resonates with entrepreneurs across the country, Chris is a  sought-after speaker for many major companies and trade industries, and the associated organizations that are dedicated to serving the transition and growth needs of business owners. He built his career as a key value growth integrator for major companies, including The Sherwin Williams Company, FedEx Logistics, Nike, Dell, and Textron. Finding passion in changing middle market business owners' lives through rapid growth projects, Chris emerged a game-changer, noting a milestone project with a family-owned private company that he helped grow from $90 million to over $240 million in three years and successfully selling to a multi-national strategic buyer. Now with a wealth of experience and a proven value acceleration system, Chris has established a family investment company with his son, with ownership stakes in eight lower middle market businesses.

FOR BUSINESS OWNERS. BY A BUSINESS OWNER.

Walking to Destiny is not only your essential resource to understand what makes your business attractive and ready for transition; it is a business owner's handbook to learn how to rapidly grow value and ultimately unlock the personal wealth trapped in your most significant financial asset: *your business.*

ORDER MORE COPIES OF
WALKING TO DESTINY

"An essential resource for understanding what makes your business attractive and ready for transition."

Name: _____

Address: _____

City: _____ State/Province: _____

Zip/Postal Code: _____ Phone: _____

Email: _____

Ship to (if different from above):

Name: _____

Address: _____

City: _____ State/Province: _____

Zip/Postal Code: _____ Phone: _____

Email: _____

Quantity Ordered: _____ x $32.00(hardback) / $21.95(paperback) = _____

Credit Card Type: _____ Visa _____ MasterCard _____

Credit Card #: _____

Expiration Date: _____

Name on Card: _____

Signature for Credit Card: _____